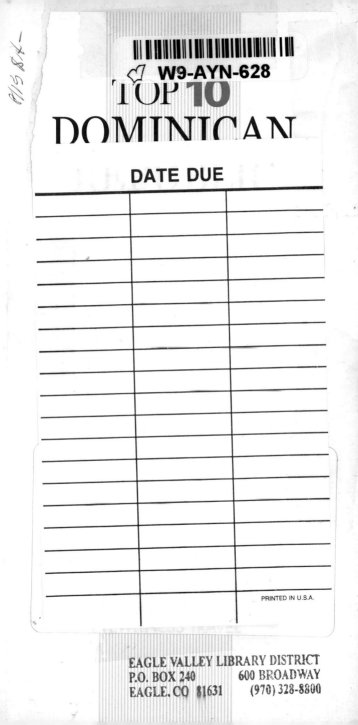

W9-AYN-628

TOP 10
DOMINICAN

DATE DUE

		PRINTED IN U.S.A.

Contents

Left **Windsurfing, Cabarete** Center **Church, La Romana** Right **Victorian houses, Puerto Plata**

LONDON, NEW YORK,
MELBOURNE, MUNICH AND DELHI
www.dk.com

Printed and bound in China

First American Edition, 2005
15 16 17 18 10 9 8 7 6 5 4 3 2 1

Published in the United States by DK Publishing,
345 Hudson Street, New York, New York 10014

**Reprinted with revisions 2006, 2009, 2011,
2013, 2015**
Copyright 2005, 2015
© Dorling Kindersley Limited, London
A Penguin Random House Company

Published in Great Britain by
Dorling Kindersley Limited.

A catalog record for this book is available
from the Library of Congress.

ISSN 1479-344X
ISBN 978-1-46542-963-6

Within each Top 10 list in this book, no hierarchy
of quality or popularity is implied. All 10 are,
in the editor's opinion, of roughly equal merit.

MIX
Paper from
responsible sources
FSC™ C018179

Contents

Dominican Republic's Top 10

The information in this DK Eyewitness Top 10 Travel Guide is checked regularly.
Every effort has been made to ensure that this book is as up-to-date as possible at the time of
going to press. Some details, however, such as telephone numbers, opening hours, prices,
gallery hanging arrangements and travel information, are liable to change. The publishers
cannot accept responsibility for any consequences arising from the use of this book, nor for
any material on third party websites, and cannot guarantee that any website address in this
book will be a suitable source of travel information. We value the views and suggestions of our
readers very highly. Please write to: Publisher, DK Eyewitness Travel Guides, Dorling Kindersley,
80 Strand, London, Great Britain WC2R 0RL, or email: travelguides@dk.com.

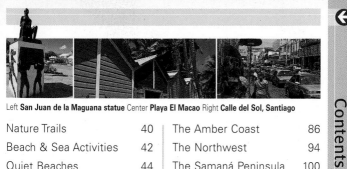

Left **San Juan de la Maguana statue** Center **Playa El Macao** Right **Calle del Sol, Santiago**

Left **Exhibits outside Museo de Arte, Bonao** Right **Boaters near El Morro**

DOMINICAN REPUBLIC'S TOP 10

DOMINICAN REPUBLIC'S TOP 10

TOP 10 Dominican Republic Highlights

The Dominican Republic is a country of surprising contrasts and extraordinary variety. From the chilly peak of the Caribbean's highest mountain to some of the region's most delightful beaches, the country boasts lush valleys, spectacular waterfalls, and sun-baked deserts. The past and present also blend in a fascinating mix of colonial buildings and modern hotels, sleepy rural villages and lively tourist resorts. The people, too, reflect a kaleidoscope of influences – Spanish, African, indigenous – creating a culture that emphasizes both creativity and fun in the fields of music, sport, and art.

1 Santo Domingo: The Zona Colonial

The historic jewel in the capital's crown, this district of restored colonial buildings and shady plazas is filled with well-preserved reminders of a bygone age *(see pp8–9)*.

2 Santo Domingo: The Modern City

The modern metropolis encompasses crowded downtown streets, charming suburbs, and relaxing parks, where art galleries rub shoulders with US-style shopping malls *(see pp10–11)*.

3 Constanza & "The Dominican Alps"

Only two hours from the capital, the rugged interior is a walker's paradise of green meadows and clear rivers, surrounded by pine forests and mountains. Pico Duarte, the highest mountain in the Caribbean, lies here *(see pp12–13)*.

4 Santiago

The laid-back second city is different in ambience from bustling Santo Domingo. Its streets are filled with monuments to its past glories as a tobacco boom town *(see pp14–15)*.

Previous pages **View from the balcony of Alcázar de Colón to Calle Las Damas, Santo Domingo**

5 Puerto Plata

Steeped in colonial history, the North Coast port is also the hub for the area's thriving tourist complexes, offering both sightseeing and entertainment. Tourist attractions include the San Felipe Fortress, Parque Central with La Glorieta, and Museo del Ambar *(see pp16–17)*.

AMBER MUSEUM

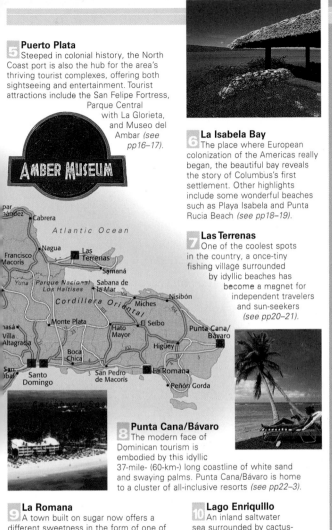

6 La Isabela Bay

The place where European colonization of the Americas really began, the beautiful bay reveals the story of Columbus's first settlement. Other highlights include some wonderful beaches such as Playa Isabela and Punta Rucia Beach *(see pp18–19)*.

7 Las Terrenas

One of the coolest spots in the country, a once-tiny fishing village surrounded by idyllic beaches has become a magnet for independent travelers and sun-seekers *(see pp20–21)*.

8 Punta Cana/Bávaro

The modern face of Dominican tourism is embodied by this idyllic 37-mile- (60-km-) long coastline of white sand and swaying palms. Punta Cana/Bávaro is home to a cluster of all-inclusive resorts *(see pp22–3)*.

9 La Romana

A town built on sugar now offers a different sweetness in the form of one of the country's most luxurious resorts, Casa de Campo, and an unforgettable transplant from Italy, Altos de Chavón *(see pp24–5)*.

10 Lago Enriquillo

An inland saltwater sea surrounded by cactus-studded wilderness, this natural wonder involves a boat trip and close encounters with crocodiles and tame giant iguanas *(see pp26–7)*.

🔟 Santo Domingo: The Zona Colonial

The Zona Colonial is the historic heart of Santo Domingo. This square mile of pretty streets and shady squares contains some of the oldest colonial buildings in the Western Hemisphere, including the cathedral. To walk along the Calle de las Damas is to retrace the steps of the first Spanish explorers, who used Santo Domingo as a base for the conquest of Latin America. Yet this district is no museum piece. It's dotted with shops, restaurants, and cafés, many housed in colonial-era buildings. It is also a real neighborhood, where families sit outside their homes enjoying the cool of the evening.

Straw hats for sale at Parque Colón

⊙ The bustling Café El Conde, on the corner of Parque Colón, may not be the most luxurious establishment in town, but is ideal for a cold drink, snack or simple meal.

⊘ Shorts and swimwear are not suitable for the city center, especially in churches and the Pantheon. Even poor Dominicans dress smartly, and they expect the same from visitors.

• Map N3
• Torre del Homenaje: Fortaleza Ozama; Open 9am–4pm Mon–Sat, 10am–4pm Sun; Adm US$1
• The National Pantheon: Open 10am–5pm daily; Free
• Alcázar de Colón: Open 9am–5pm Tue–Sun; Adm US$3
• Casa del Cordón (located in the Banco Popular): Open 8am–3pm Mon–Fri; Courtyard only; Free

Top 10 Sights

1 The Cathedral
2 Torre del Homenaje
3 Parque Colón
4 Calle de las Damas
5 The National Pantheon
6 Hostal Nicolás de Ovando
7 Las Atarazanas
8 Alcázar de Colón
9 Las Casas Reales
10 Casa del Cordón

The Cathedral
This exuberant mix of Gothic and Classical influences *(above)* dates back to 1540. It has survived earthquakes and pirate attacks, and was reputedly the original resting place of Christopher Columbus. Its cool, dark interior contains magnificent monuments.

Torre del Homenaje
Built as a watchtower in 1503, Homage Tower *(right)* was used to sight approaching pirate raiders, but later served as a prison, even during Trujillo's dictatorship *(see p31)*.

Parque Colón
Named after Columbus, the large open space is dominated by a grandiose statue of the explorer *(below)*. The square's cafés are a good point for people-watching.

Calle de las Damas
A medieval thoroughfare lined with museums and churches, this street contains some of the old city's most tastefully restored buildings.

The National Pantheon

Formerly a Jesuit church, this Neo-Classical building commemorates the country's national heroes. A solemn atmosphere fills the large marble-lined interior, and a uniformed soldier stands guard over the eternal flame.

Hostal Nicolás de Ovando

This hotel *(left)* is set within the mansion of the colony's first governor and features the original balconies and Andalusian fountain. A great place to stay, with views of the Ozama River.

Las Atarazanas

A line of former warehouses, converted into shops and restaurants *(left)*. The 16th-century buildings are linked by pleasant courtyards. The Calle Las Atarazanas ends in the Puerta Las Atarazanas, in front of the cruise harbor.

Alcázar de Colón

The stately 2-story palace *(above)* built by Christopher Columbus's son, Diego, overlooks the river and the large Plaza España. This Moorish-influenced coral-stone mansion is Santo Domingo's most impressive colonial site.

Las Casas Reales

The Real Audiencia or Supreme Court once sat in this early 16th-century mansion, now a colonial museum. Look out for the *reloj del sol* (sundial), reputedly placed for judges to check the time.

Casa del Cordón

The House of the Rope *(right)* is said to be the first 2-story building in the Americas. Diego Columbus lived here while his palace was being built. Its façade is decorated by a chiseled sash-and-cord motif.

Drake's Destruction

Colonial Santo Domingo's heyday came to an abrupt end in 1586 when Sir Francis Drake's 20-strong fleet sailed upriver. Unopposed, the English indulged in a month-long orgy of looting and demolition, while the Protestant Sir Francis slung his hammock in the cathedral. Santo Domingo was ruined.

TOP10 Santo Domingo: The Modern City

Beyond the Zona Colonial is a fast-moving metropolis of almost three million people, where upmarket suburbs rub shoulders with bleak-looking shantytowns and where quiet parks and museums provide a respite from the capital's frenetic traffic. The city radiates inland from the river and coastline, moving from compact 19th-century barrios to the spread-out commercial districts of the modern uptown. Spanish and Caribbean influences, expressed in wrought-iron balconies and ornate gingerbread-style woodcarving, give way to functional concrete office blocks and suburbs.

Statue of Parque Mirador del Sur

Carriage at Malecón

🌐 On the corner of Calle El Conde and Calle Hostos, the Mercure Comercial hotel offers an air-conditioned bar and other facilities.

🕐 To request a free tour of the Palacio Nacional (Tue–Fri), call 809 695 8359. Permission takes 15 working days, and you are expected to look suitably dressed.

- Map E4
- Los Tres Ojos: Mirador del Este Park; Open 9am–5pm daily; Adm US$2
- Museo del Hombre Dominicano: Plaza de la Cultura; 809 687 3622; Open 10am–5pm Tue–Sun; Adm US$3
- Palacio de Bellas Artes: Máximo Gómez & Independencia; 809 687 0504; Free
- Botanic Garden: Av República Colombia; 809 385 2611; Open 9am–5pm daily; Adm US$5
- Columbus Lighthouse: Open 10am–5pm daily; Adm US$3

Top 10 Sights

1. The Malecón
2. Ciudad Nueva
3. Los Tres Ojos
4. Gazcue
5. Museo del Hombre Dominicano
6. Palacio Nacional
7. Palacio de Bellas Artes
8. Botanic Garden
9. Parque Mirador del Sur
10. Columbus Lighthouse (Faro a Colón)

2 Ciudad Nueva
Next to the Zona Colonial, this low-level neighborhood of narrow streets and plazas contains fine examples of 19th-century architecture and maintains the atmosphere of a traditional *barrio*.

1 The Malecón
Stretching several miles eastwards from the port, the Malecón – also known as Avenida George Washington – is the city's breezy seafront boulevard, lined with high-rise hotels, restaurants, and bars *(above & p52)*.

3 Los Tres Ojos
This impressive 50-ft (15-m) limestone cave is located in the Mirador del Este Park. At night the caves are illuminated. Visitors have the option of either taking a walking tour or exploring the cave by boat.

4 Gazcue
A leafy middle-class suburb dating from the 1930s, Gazcue's eccentric mix of buildings includes imitation chalets and half-timbered English-style architecture and a number of cafés and galleries.

5 Museo del Hombre Dominicano
Part of the Modernist 1970s Plaza de la Cultura complex, this collection of artifacts reveals the day-to-day life and rituals of the pre-Columbian Taino people *(right & p34)*.

9 Parque Mirador del Sur
A haven for joggers and walkers, this park is located in the affluent diplomatic district. The limestone cliffs on the southern edge contain a series of caves, one of which houses a restaurant and another a vast discotheque.

10 Columbus Lighthouse (Faro a Colón)
Inaugurated in 1992 to celebrate the 500th anniversary of Columbus's arrival, this marble-clad monument *(above)* attracted criticism as a waste of money. But the sheer scale of the cross-shaped edifice is impressive. It is also the site of Columbus's tomb.

6 Palacio Nacional
Although the presidential palace *(above)* looks impregnable, you can visit this 1940s exercise in Neo-Classical pomp, with its mahogany furniture and hall of mirrors. It houses government departments.

7 Palacio de Bellas Artes
An austere Neo-Classical façade announces the aesthetic credentials of the city's Beaux-Arts headquarters. Decorating the stairway are murals by José Vela Zanetti.

8 Botanic Garden
In the northern suburb of Arroyo Hondo, the 450-acre (182 ha) garden *(above)* showcases the tropical wealth of the country's flora, featuring palms, a Japanese garden, and 300 varieties of orchid.

Gleave's Lighthouse
JL Gleave, a 24-year-old Manchester architecture student, beat over 450 rival designs in 1929 in an international competition to commemorate Columbus's landfall. Funds for construction failed to materialize, and work began in 1986, 20 years after Gleave died.

TOP 10 Constanza & "The Dominican Alps"

The cool uplands of the country's interior are a world apart, barely 50 miles (80 km) away from the tropical heat of Santo Domingo. Dominated by the towering Cordillera Central, the mountain range that forms the island's spine, the central region is a nature-lover's paradise of protected national parks, streams, and valleys. The gentle climate encourages crops such as strawberries, and at high altitudes frosts are not uncommon. The green meadows and pine forests are far from the usual image of the Caribbean, and Pico Duarte, the highest mountain in the Caribbean, dominates the scene.

Strawberries

The 30-mile (47-km) road between Jarabacoa and Constanza makes for a fabulous drive with stunning views.

There are few gas stations on the lonely mountain roads around Jarabacoa and Constanza, so motorists should remember to fill up in town.

- Map C3
- Rancho Baiguate: 809 574 6890; www.ranchobaiguate.com
- Salto de Jimenoa: Open 8am–6pm daily; Adm US$2
- Salto de Baiguate: Open 8am–6pm daily; Free
- Parque Nacional Armando Bermúdez: Open 8am–6pm daily; Adm US$4; Official guide compulsory

Top 10 Sights

1. Jarabacoa
2. Balneario La Confluencia
3. Rancho Baiguate
4. Salto de Jimenoa
5. Salto de Baiguate
6. Constanza
7. Parque Nacional Armando Bermúdez
8. Reserva Científica Valle Nueva
9. Salto Agua Blanca
10. Pico Duarte

1 Jarabacoa
Once an isolated agricultural village, this small town has become a popular summer retreat and a base for walkers and sports enthusiasts. The Río Yaque del Norte runs close to town, tempting swimmers and rafters *(see p40)*.

2 Balneario La Confluencia
Jarabacoa's own natural swimming pool *(below)* was formed where the Yaque del Norte meets the Jimenoa just outside town. The water can be quite fast-moving when the rivers are high, and there is also a shady wooded park.

3 Rancho Baiguate
The best-organized adventure center in the area, this rustic complex *(above)* is set in attractive riverside grounds and offers a range of outings and activities as well as accommodation, a swimming pool, and a Dominican art gallery. Day visitors are welcome.

4 Salto de Jimenoa

This 131-ft (40-m) waterfall is reached via a series of hair-raisingly narrow suspension bridges. The cold water of the Río Yaque del Norte cascades noisily into a deep pool. Lush vegetation completely surrounds the rocky canyon. Swimming is not allowed.

5 Salto de Baiguate

A scenic walk around a path cut into the edge of a ravine leads down to the valley floor where a torrent of water crashes into a swimming hole *(left)*, which is best reached on horseback.

6 Constanza

Set in a fertile valley ringed by mountains *(left)*, the town of Constanza is an excellent starting point for hikes. The heart of the region's agricultural economy, it has a busy farmer's market.

7 Parque Nacional Armando Bermúdez

The 289 sq-mile (750 sq-km) reserve *(above)* in the Cordillera Central is home to a stunning array of flora and fauna. The ranger station at La Ciénaga is one of the major starting points for organized treks.

8 Reserva Científica Valle Nueva

The pot-holed and vertiginous mountain road from Constanza to San José de Ocoa traverses this remote protected zone, where impenetrable pine forests offer protection to countless species of birds.

9 Salto Agua Blanca

A long trek through rough mountainous terrain is amply rewarded by this spectacular 492-ft (150-m) waterfall, whose white water drops straight down into a pool. Ferns and other vegetation cling onto the sheer rock faces of the canyon.

10 Pico Duarte

Not officially climbed until 1944 and named after the father of independence, the peak is often shrouded in cloud. Visitors can also admire the mountain from a distance *(left & p40)*.

Japanese Dominicans

In the 1950s, President Trujillo imported 200 Japanese farming families to form an agricultural colony in Constanza and boost the town's economy. The arrangement was meant to be temporary, but many of the families stayed on. Some of their descendants still live in the area, and a Japanese social club thrives.

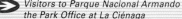

Visitors to Parque Nacional Armando Bermúdez must register at the Park Office at La Ciénaga

🔟 Santiago

Santiago de los Caballeros (Santiago of the Gentlemen) *is the Dominican Republic's second-largest city. From its founding in 1495 by the 30 Spanish noblemen* (caballeros)*, this busy metropolis has considered itself richer and more industrious than the capital. Set in the fertile Cibao Valley, Santiago has historically been the hub of the country's agricultural wealth, and its millionaire families largely owe their fortunes to the sugar and tobacco grown nearby. The city is calmer than Santo Domingo, but lively enough in Calle del Sol and around the landmark Monument to the Heroes.*

Calle del Sol

🟢 Santiago's most attractive cafés and restaurants are clustered around Calle del Sol. At weekends the surrounding area often becomes an open-air disco, with loud music.

🟢 For marvelous views of Santiago and the Cibao Valley, dine on the terrace of Rancho Camp David *(see p56)* and enjoy the sparkling lights at night.

• Map C2
• Palacio Consistorial: Open 8am–5pm Mon–Fri; Free
• Museo del Tabaco "La Aurora": Open 8am–5pm Mon–Fri; Free
• Monumento a los Héroes de la Restauración: Open 8am–5pm Mon–Sat; Free (guide US$5)
• Museo Folklórico Don Tomás Morel: Open 9am–noon, 2–6pm Mon–Fri; Donation requested

Top 10 Sights

1. Parque Duarte
2. Cathedral
3. Centro de Recreo
4. Calle del Sol
5. Palacio Consistorial
6. Mercado Modelo
7. Monumento a los Héroes de la Restauración
8. Museo del Tabaco "La Aurora"
9. Gran Teatro del Cibao
10. Museo Folklórico Don Tomás Morel

Parque Duarte
The heart of old Santiago, this pleasantly tree-filled space is a meeting place for locals and a good spot for people-watching *(above)*. You can hire a horse-drawn carriage for a tour of the surrounding streets, or buy a merengue CD.

1839–1897

Cathedral
The Catedral Santiago Apóstol *(left)* dates from the late 19th century, but the most eye-catching features are the modern stained-glass windows. Ulíses Heureaux *(see p31)*, one of the country's dictatorial presidents (who was local to the area), lies here in a marble tomb.

Centro de Recreo
Offering an unexpectedly exotic Moorish flavor, the Mudéjar-style private club testifies to the wealth of Santiago's 1890s sugar barons. An ornate façade of arches and pillars conceals an opulent interior of carved wooden ceilings and a grand ballroom.

Calle del Sol
The buzzing urban thoroughfare of Santiago, this street is lined with department stores, hotels, and sidewalk vendors. At night, shoppers and office workers give way to those in search of entertainment in its many bars and restaurants (see p55).

Palacio Consistorial
A proud civic structure, formerly the town hall, this fine example of Victorian-era Neo-Classical symmetry houses the city's museum and art gallery.

Mercado Modelo
A smaller equivalent of Santo Domingo's cavernous covered market (above), the green and white structure dates from the 1940s.

Monumento a los Héroes de la Restauración
The Monument to the Heroes (left) boasts a 230-ft (70-m) pillar topped by an allegorical figure of Victory. The marble edifice was commissioned by Trujillo and contains murals by Vela Zanetti, inspired by Mexican Diego Rivera.

Museo del Tabaco "La Aurora"
This reproduction of Santiago's oldest cigar factory, "La Aurora", is in the garden of Centro León (see p34). Visitors learn how the crop is grown and how cigars are rolled (below).

Gran Teatro del Cibao
Another monumental folly, the modern marble-clad theater is the 1980s legacy of President Balaguer (see p31), responsible also for Santo Domingo's Columbus Lighthouse. Its huge auditorium stages occasional opera.

Museo Folklórico Don Tomás Morel
Founded by carnival promoter, artist, and poet Tomás Morel in 1962, this delightful museum is packed with colorful carnival masks and religious icons as well as more everyday items used in the past. There's also a traditional Dominican kitchen on display.

Liberation Struggles
Santiago played a crucial part in the struggle to oust the Spanish in 1863 after they had annexed the country. A force of over 6,000 guerrillas besieged the Spanish garrison until they surrendered. A provisional government was set up in Santiago, but not before the city was almost destroyed by fire.

Centro de Recreo is a private club and usually closed to visitors, but members may show you around if you're appropriately dressed

Puerto Plata

The "Silver Port" lies between the glittering Atlantic Ocean and the imposing bulk of the Pico Isabel de Torres. Its roots go back to 1495, but it was during the 1970s that this once-sleepy provincial back-water was rejuvenated by the advent of mass tourism. The nearby resorts of Playa Dorada and Sosúa attract legions of visitors each year, but a tour of Puerto Plata's colorful center, complete with Victorian-era architecture, galleries, and restaurants should not be missed. A tight grid of central streets dates to the brief tobacco boom in the 19th century. This is the best place to soak up the atmosphere of a bygone golden age.

Artifacts at the Museum of Taino Art

🍽 Check out the café at the **Museo de General Gregorio Luperón** for refreshments.

🚡 The cable car can be closed in bad weather and has a long wait in peak seasons. Check with your hotel before setting out.

• Map C1 • San Felipe Fortress: Open 9am–5pm Tue–Sun; Adm US$5
• Museum of Taino Art: Open 9am–6pm Mon–Fri; Free • Museo de General Gregorio Luperón: 809 261 8661; Open 10am–5pm Tue–Sun; Adm US$3 • Museo del Ambar: Open 9am–6pm Mon–Sat; Adm US$2
• Brugal Rum Factory: Open 9–11am, 2–4pm Mon–Fri; Free • Cable Car: 809 970 0435; Open 9am–5pm daily; Adm US$10

Top 10 Sights

1. San Felipe Fortress
2. Museo de General Gregorio Luperón
3. Parque Central
4. La Glorieta
5. Museum of Taino Art
6. San Felipe Cathedral
7. Museo del Ambar
8. Brugal Rum Factory
9. Pico Isabel de Torres
10. Cable Car

San Felipe Fortress
A solid-looking bastion *(right)* intended to deter marauding pirates in the 16th century, this brick-built fort – the oldest in the New World – has been restored and contains cannon and other weaponry from the colonial period in a small museum. You can also climb the towers and gun turrets.

Museo de General Gregorio Luperón
Dedicated to independence hero General Gregorio Luperón, this museum walks you through his life and the history of 19th-century Puerto Plata. Period artifacts and the General's belongings are housed in an elegantly restored Victorian-era building. There are multi-lingual tours, and a lift for the disabled.

Parque Central
A shaded oasis, *(above)* surrounded by whitewashed Victorian architecture, this is the heart of old Puerto Plata and a pleasant place to sit in a café or park bench. Most of the town's quaint gingerbread buildings are clustered around the park.

La Glorieta
This 1960s reconstruction of the original gazebo *(below)* provides the focal point of the square. The symmetrical two-story white-and-green wooden bandstand was apparently constructed to a Belgian blueprint in 1872.

5 Museum of Taino Art
Part of a large complex of art and handicrafts called Plaza Arawak, this collection of pre-Columbian artifacts explores the mysterious religious beliefs of the island's indigenous people.

6 San Felipe Cathedral
Given a facelift after the September 2003 earthquake, the twin-towered Catedral San Felipe Apóstol *(above)* is a successful blend of traditional colonial style and Art Deco influences.

9 Pico Isabel de Torres
The 2,600-ft (793-m) peak offers a stunning bird's-eye view over the town and coastline. A smaller version of Rio's statue of Christ gazes protectively over the horizon, while a Botanic Garden makes for a pleasant stroll.

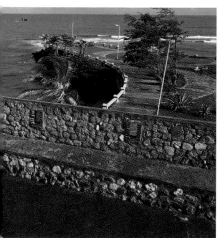

10 Cable Car
The *teleférico (above)* is the most spectacular way of reaching the summit: a smooth 20-minute ride up the Caribbean's only cable car system, over the wooded mountainside, with terrific views of Puerto Plata and the Atlantic Ocean.

8 Brugal Rum Factory
A tour of the 1880s rum bottling plant reveals the extent of Dominicans' love affair with rum *(below)*. The production lines are an impressive sight, but the highlight is the gratis cocktail.

7 Museo del Ambar
Housed in a German tobacco magnate's exquisite mansion, the museum *(above)* showcases the local amber industry, displaying finely crafted jewelry as well as natural phenomena such as a million-year-old lizard trapped in a luminous block of the precious resin.

Tobacco Boom
A sudden upturn in world tobacco prices transformed sleepy Puerto Plata's fortunes in the 1870s, and the port became a magnet to merchants, including several German entrepreneurs, who traded in Cibao-grown tobacco. Their opulent dwellings, many now sadly dilapidated, are testimony to an age when this was the Caribbean's richest town.

Dominican Republic's Top 10

AMBER MUSEUM

Bahía de Puerto Plata

⓾ La Isabela Bay

Set among some of the country's most rugged countryside and bordered by magnificent beaches, La Isabela breathes history as the site of the first permanent colonial settlement in the Americas. The bay protects a placid expanse of ocean, while a pristine white beach looks much as it must have done in 1493 when Christopher Columbus decided to establish a town on this spot, named in honor of the Spanish Queen. The excavated ruins of La Isabela give a powerful impression of that decisive moment, but it is the situation as much as the archeological display that makes this place special. An adventurous trek through remote terrain is rewarded by an unforgettable insight into how the course of history was changed.

Parque Nacional Histórico La Isabela

🗘 "Official" guides from the national park office are meant to accompany visitors. They will expect a tip.

The roads around La Isabela are potholed and often occupied by large herds of goats. Driving after dark is therefore not a good idea.

• Map B1
• Parque Nacional Histórico La Isabela: Open 8am–6pm Mon–Sat; Adm US$4
• Museum: Open 8am–6pm Mon–Sat; Free
• Templo de las Américas: Open 9am–5pm daily; Free
• Cayo Paraiso: Tours offered by tour operators such as Paraiso Tours depart from Punta Rucia on Tue, Thu, Sat & Sun: 809 320 7606; Price US$50

Top 10 Sights

1. Museum
2. The Settlement
3. Columbus's House
4. Cemetery
5. Parque Nacional Histórico La Isabela
6. Playa Isabela
7. Templo de las Américas
8. Laguna Estero Hondo
9. Punta Rucia Beach
10. Cayo Paraiso

Museum
1️⃣ The park's museum contains a compact but well-maintained display of Taino artifacts *(below)*, including pottery and arrowheads. The captions are Spanish-only, but the exhibits are visually interesting and include a model of Columbus's ship, the *Santa Maria*.

The Settlement
2️⃣ Small walls of roughly hewn limestone *(right)* trace the foundations of La Isabela's structures, including what are thought to be warehouses, a chapel, a rudimentary hospital, and a watchtower.

Columbus's House
3️⃣ On a slight bluff overlooking the site is the shell of the residence belonging to Columbus. Covered with a thatched awning, the ruin *(above)* shows that he lived in a modest dwelling made of packed earth and stone.

Cemetery
The New World's first Christian cemetery *(above)* occupies a scenic waterside position, and is decorated by the later addition of white crosses. Both Spanish and Taino people were buried here and exhumed.

Playa Isabela
The beach, where the slow-moving Bajabonico River meets the sea, is an unspoilt stretch of sand, where tiny fishing boats bob offshore. Amenities are few, so come prepared *(right & p44)*.

Templo de las Américas
This colonial-style church *(below)* is a blend of whitewashed stone and brick, built in 1990, in time to celebrate the 500th anniversary of Columbus's arrival. Pope John Paul II said Mass here in 1992.

Punta Rucia Beach
This is a long expanse of soft-white sand and limpid water, where small restaurants and shops provide cold drinks and freshly caught fish.

Cayo Paraiso
A tiny speck of sun-bleached circular sand-bank surrounded by coral reef and aquamarine sea, the cay can be visited on an organized tour by speedboat from Punta Rucia or the village of Castillo.

Parque Nacional Histórico La Isabela
A protected national park gradually excavated since the 1950s, the site of the original settlement sits on a promontory; an expanse of red sand dotted with acacia trees and criss-crossed by paths that lead visitors around the architectural remains *(below)*.

Laguna Estero Hondo
You can explore one of the region's best-preserved mangrove forests with a boat trip through this wild lagoon. Gnarled mangrove thickets are home to many birds, and you may be fortunate enough to catch sight of a rare manatee *(see p67)*.

Trujillo's Blunder
La Isabela's archeological potential was recognized by the Dominican dictator Trujillo, but when he ordered workmen to tidy up the site in 1952 they were rather too zealous and reportedly bulldozed much of the remains into the sea. Locals and souvenir-hunters have also been responsible for removing valuable artifacts.

⒑ Las Terrenas

One of the Dominican Republic's most sought-after tourist areas, Las Terrenas was a tiny ramshackle fishing village until the 1980s when the town was redeveloped. An influx of expatriates from North America and Europe has brought a wide array of guesthouses and restaurants. But development has not ruined this welcoming seaside community's relaxed atmosphere. Lying on the North Coast of the Samaná Peninsula, a lush strip of land pushing out into the Atlantic, the town is blessed by the proximity of some of the country's most beautiful beaches and by spectacular countryside around. Extensive groves of coconut trees fringe expanses of white sand which slope gently and invitingly into clear warm water.

Painted walls of a beachside restaurant

⭑ ATMs in the village are sometimes empty, especially at weekends and towards the end of the month. Make sure you have enough cash before you arrive.

Although attractive, coconut trees are dangerous, and injuries are known to occur from falling nuts. Avoid sitting directly below.

• Map F2
• Tourist office: Carretera Las Terrenas, 809 240 6363; Open 8:30am–3pm Mon–Fri
• Profundo Blue Diving Center, Hotel Aligio; 829 349 1913; www.profundoblue.com
• Turtle Dive Center; 829 903 0659 www.turtledivecenter. com
• The Beach Restaurant; Playa Coson, 809 847 3288
• Gran Bahía Principe El Portillo: 809 240 6100

Top 10 Attractions

⒈ Playa Las Terrenas

Stretching a mile (1.6 km) in either direction from the small town center, the attractive beach *(right)* is clean and safe with ample shade. Heading westwards, Playa Cacao, close to small hotels and bars, is slightly more developed than the others.

⒉ Diving

Relatively unspoilt coral reefs lie close to Las Terrenas. Divers *(above)* are attracted to nearby Playa Las Ballenas, where a group of small islands stand just offshore. There are dive shops, such as Profundo Blue Diving Center, and snorkel hire shops.

⒊ Beachside Restaurants

Spread along the beach either side of the main intersection are many top-rate but informal fish eateries *(below)*. Fish with coconut is recommended. Early evenings are atmospheric with technicolor sunsets over the water.

Haitian Art
Naïve Haitian art is widely available and is often mediocre and mass-produced. The Haitian Caraïbes Art Gallery *(below)* has a good and reasonably-priced selection of wooden sculptures and voodoo-influenced images.

Shopping
For a small town, Las Terrenas offers a surprising range of shopping opportunities, from the small modern mall to outlets along the main street. Bargains can be had by bartering with stall-holders, especially near the beaches.

Gran Bahía Principe El Portillo
Great service and the exclusive use of paradisal beach El Portillo are the hallmarks of this elegant hotel and resort. Sporting options such as windsurfing, kayaking, tennis, and volleyball are also offered *(above)*.

Salto de Limón
A 130-ft (40-m) cascade of white water *(above)* ends up in a delightfully clear pool, reached by a one-hour horseback ride from El Limón village. The trek to this remote waterfall is through beautiful and fertile countryside.

Playa Bonita
The immaculate "Beautiful Beach" is fringed by coconut trees, in which guesthouses are hidden. Less crowded than Las Terrenas, and ideal for kids *(left & p44)*.

Playa Cosón
This isolated curve of powdery white sand, clear water, and palm groves looks every bit the idyllic image of the tourist brochures. A couple of fishermen's shacks sell cold drinks and grilled fish to this beach's few visitors.

Nightlife
Las Terrenas is rightly celebrated for its busy but laid-back after-dark ambience, particularly at weekends when locals and tourists mingle at an open-air street fair or visit its many bars.

A Growing Resort
The transformation of Las Terrenas from a remote fishing community to a thriving tourism center was fueled by the French, Canadians, Swiss, and Germans, who fell in love with the place in the 1980s and invested in real estate and accommodation. The village's isolation was ended by the opening of a paved local road and a motorway.

TOP 10 Punta Cana/Bávaro

The east coast, with its reef-protected white beaches and placid waters, is the country's undisputed tourist mecca. Some 40 miles (64 km) of uninterrupted beach sweeps up the southeastern tip of the country, the endless vistas of sea, sand, and coconut trees broken only by clusters of low-level hotels and villas. Since the 1980s a bonanza of construction has seen huge self-contained tourist cities rise up along the water's edge and the area has also become a popular place for expatriates and Dominicans to live. It is home to Cap Cana, a luxury resort with one of the Caribbean's biggest inland marina. It is possible, should you wish, to escape the luxury of the hotel enclave and to explore the beaches – some calm, others wild – that stretch as far as the eye can see.

Relaxing by the beach

⚠ It is possible to get burned even on a cloudy day, so take all due precautions and be sure to wear adequate sunblock in the daytime.

Check the quality of the glass-bottom boat before paying for a trip, as there have been complaints in some cases that the "glass" is hard-to-see-through plastic.

• Map H4
• *Indigenous Eyes Ecological Park and Reserve: 809 959 9221; www.puntacana. org/reserve*
• *Dolphin World: 809 468 2000; Open 8am–6pm daily; Adm adults US$35, children US$25; Dolphin swims from US$109; www. dolphinexplorer.com.do*

Top 10 Sights

1. Playa Punta Cana
2. Indigenous Eyes Ecological Park and Reserve
3. Bávaro Beach Hotels
4. Dolphin World
5. Bávaro Bazaar
6. Water Sports
7. Cortecito Beach
8. Horseback Riding
9. Playa Macao
10. Boca de Maimón

Playa Punta Cana
Backed by the landscaped grounds of two huge resorts, this long strip of perfect sand leads into warm turquoise water *(right)*. Coconut trees provide shade, and only guests are allowed to use the resorts' facilities.

Indigenous Eyes Ecological Park and Reserve
This protected, 1,500-acre lowland subtropical forest is dedicated to conservation, research, and recreation. Explore the numerous trails, swim in one of the freshwater lagoons, and visit the petting zoo.

Bávaro Beach Hotels
Bigger and more developed than Punta Cana, the resort is dominated by a complex of modern hotels *(below)*, offering a plethora of restaurants, water sports, and other creature comforts. Several 18-hole golf courses provide green oases within the sun-baked sand.

Dolphin World
Swim with dolphins, brave snorkeling with sharks and stingrays, and cavort with adorable fur seals. With a focus on conservation, Dolphin World encourages learning about the animals through interaction in their natural environment. *(See also p37).*

Water Sports
The Punta Cana/Bávaro area offers many beach activities *(above)*, including diving, catamarans, and snorkeling in the limpid waters. The conditions make for excellent visibility, and glass-bottom boats reveal an underwater world of coral and fish life.

Playa Macao
An asphalt road leads northwards from the all-inclusive resorts, leaving behind the manicured sand and entering a different landscape of wild beaches, and a surfers' paradise. There are small beach-front restaurants serving fresh seafood. Swimming is not advised, except at the more protected cove at Macao *(below & p44).*

Boca de Maimón
Also known as Uvero Alto, this previously undeveloped area is now home to a number of all-inclusive hotels. Boca de Maimón is surrounded by marshes and lagoons, home to sea turtles.

Bávaro Bazaar
Peruse this Saturday morning market on Plaza Turquesa, Il Cortecito, which promotes local creativity and talent. Pick up handmade jewelry, art, and Dominican produce.

Cortecito Beach
One of the few stretches of sand not claimed by the all-inclusive giants, Cortecito has a more authentically Dominican feel, with small restaurants, bars, and a cluster of souvenir stalls. The sand is just as fine as around the big hotels.

Horseback Riding
The empty expanses of beach along the coast make this an ideal place for beginners or experienced riders to hire a horse *(left).*

Millionaire Paradise
Punta Cana and Bávaro cater to the masses, but the Costa del Coco has more exclusive, luxury resorts such as Corales, where Russian actor and dancer Mikhail Baryshnikov owns a property. There are also luxury hotels, villas, a marina, and golf courses at Cap Cana.

For more information on horseback riding **See p42**

TOP 10 La Romana

"King Sugar" still reigns in the southern port city of La Romana, a place dedicated to cutting, milling, and exporting sugar since 1917. The huge sugar mill, though damaged by 1998's Hurricane Georges, still dominates the town, and you are likely to see cane-filled trains trundling through the surrounding countryside. Tourism rather than sugar is now the town's main lifeblood, and its pride and joy is the nearby Casa de Campo resort. This tropical playground of beach, sports facilities, and exquisite gardens offers the most sophisticated choice of activities.

Teeth of the Dog golf course

🕙 Casa de Campo is theoretically guests-only, but cruise ship passengers may book horseback riding or golf sessions while onboard.

To visit Altos de Chavón, you must purchase a day pass (US$25) at the main entrance of Casa de Campo. This pass allows you to use all other public facilities, including Playa Minitas.

• Map G4
• Casa de Campo: PO Box 140, La Romana; 809 523 3333; www. casadecampo.com.do
• Teeth of the Dog: 809 523 8115; Open 8am–5pm daily; Adm US$250; Caddies & equipment hire extra
• Altos de Chavón: Daily; Adm US$25

Top 10 Sights

1. Parque Central
2. Casa de Campo
3. Mercado Municipal
4. Golf Course
5. Playa Minitas
6. Marina
7. Isla Catalina
8. Altos de Chavón
9. The Amphitheater
10. Río Chavón

Parque Central
The large and attractive square has been renovated since the hurricane and is bordered by the pretty Santa Rosa de Lima church *(above)*. This is the place for meeting the locals, and visitors can also watch the early evening streetlife.

Casa de Campo
One of the world's premier resorts, this 700-acre (283 ha) expanse of beautifully tended gardens and tasteful villas is a world away from workaday La Romana *(see p72)*. Its sports facilities are second to none, and its undeniable prestige is reflected in its prices.

Hillside village of Altos de Chavón

Mercado Municipal
This bustling market *(below)* is crammed with agricultural produce as well as handicrafts and other souvenirs of interest for visitors. The *botánicas* do not sell plants, but religious and magic items, often related to local beliefs and superstitions.

Golf Course
4 The internationally famous "Teeth of the Dog" course, with 8 holes right next to the Caribbean, is one of the region's most difficult. Day visitors are allowed to inspect *(left & p38)*.

Playa Minitas
5 A secluded strip of sand behind a coral reef, this beach is reserved for guests of Casa de Campo, although visitors are usually accepted. Those with restaurant reservations can go via the main entrance.

The Amphitheater
9 Altos de Chavón's most eye-catching feature is its 5,000-seat open-air amphitheater *(above)*, a vast limestone concert bowl inaugurated by Frank Sinatra in 1982. With Greek columns and spectacular views all around, it provides an impressive backdrop for big-name performances.

Río Chavón
10 Below Altos de Chavón, the river *(above)* moves slowly through a densely wooded gorge, where palm trees are reflected in the water. New Orleans-style paddle-boats ply this dark, enigmatic, and mysterious waterway.

Marina
6 This modern waterside complex is intended for the well-heeled yachting enthusiasts who use the marina's mooring facilities. The crescent-shaped plaza *(right)* contains several up-market cafés, restaurants (reservations required), and boutiques.

Isla Catalina
7 This tiny uninhabited island draws large crowds of excursionists from the Marina to a fine white beach, where Casa de Campo has set up tourist facilities. The diving off the North Coast is best.

Altos de Chavón
8 A bizarre replica of a Tuscan hillside village, the cluster of stone houses and plazas is both an arts center and a major tourist magnet. The imitation has attracted criticism, but many love the village's old-world air.

Birthday Gift

The grandiose mock-Italian folly of Altos de Chavón was reputedly built by the president of Gulf & Western, Charles Bluhdorn, as a birthday gift to his daughter in 1976. To this day, Dominique Bluhdorn remains associated with the village as a leading light of the Altos de Chavón Cultural Center Foundation.

🔟 Lago Enriquillo

This vast inland stretch of salt water is more like a mini-sea than a lake. Glinting in an arid plain beneath rugged mountains, it marks the lowest geographical point in the Caribbean, 132 ft (40 m) below sea level, and is said to cover about the same area as Manhattan. Home to thousands of birds, iguanas, and American crocodiles, it is a protected National Park. Yet, the lake, its main island, and surrounding villages are easy to visit, offering a very different landscape from other parts of the island. Hot, dry, and sparsely inhabited, this border country stands in fascinating contrast to the developed coastal areas.

Shop at La Descubierta

🕑 There is a flat fee payable for the boat ride, irrespective of passenger numbers, so it may be worth waiting for other visitors to share the cost. The area is also prone to flooding. When water levels get too high, boat rides are not available and lake roads can become impassable.

You cannot cross the border in a rental car. Instead, fly or take the daily bus from Santo Domingo to Port-au-Prince (*see p118*).

• Map A4
• Organized tours are available from Ecotour Barahona; 809 682 2454; www.ecotourbarahona. com; US$139 per person for guided day tour with transport and food.

Top 10 Sights

1 Lago Enriquillo
2 Boat Trips
3 Isla Cabritos
4 Bird-watching
5 Crocodiles & Iguanas
6 Las Caritas
7 La Descubierta
8 Las Barias Balneario
9 Jimaní
🔟 Border Market

2 Boat Trips
Boats set off from the National Park Office in La Azufrado, and ferry visitors to the crocodiles, which prefer the fresh water inlets on the northern shore. Boatmen try to pass as close as possible to the sleepy beasts.

3 Isla Cabritos
A sandy spit of land with dry shrub and coral-strewn beaches, the Goat Island *(above)* provides perfect sanctuary to an iguana colony and some 500 crocodiles. However, when the lake rises, the island can be underwater and so cannot be visited.

1 Lago Enriquillo
Girdled by a circular road, the huge lake stands under the intense sun. Dead tree trunks emerging from the water's edge testify to its saltiness and give it an eerie atmosphere, emphasized by the silence around *(above & p110)*.

4 Bird-watching
This remote site is a haven for over 60 species of birds, many of which can be observed from the road or the water itself. The most identifiable are the flamingos *(left)*, which gather in huge numbers at dawn and dusk.

Las Caritas is a wild, open cave, with no fixed times or admission charges

Crocodiles & Iguanas
Crocodiles can be secretive, especially when the heat rises and they take to the water, but the Ricord's iguanas are not shy, approaching visitors in the hope of a snack. Feeding these large reptiles is discouraged.

Jimaní
The spread-out town of Jimaní marks one of the official border crossings into Haiti, although the frontier line is actually 3 miles (5 km) away down a very hot road. You are likely to see brightly painted Haitian buses *(above)*, known locally as *tap-taps*.

Border Market
The dusty no-man's land between the two countries is the scene of a semi-permanent out-door market, in which Haitian traders sell mostly counterfeit clothing and watches. Haiti's celebrated Barbancourt rum *(right)* is worth buying.

Las Caritas
Easily found off the side of the road near the village of Postrer Río, an open cave reveals traces of early indigenous culture and religious ritual in the form of small faces *(caritas)* carved into the coral rock.

La Descubierta
A small and sleepy outpost of single-story houses, some brightly painted, the village stands in the middle of the hot plain. It has a shaded central square, a couple of short walking paths, and several cheap bars and restaurants.

Las Barias Balneario
A strange feature of La Descubierta is its cold natural pool of slightly sulfurous water *(above)*. Popular with local families, this *balneario*, with food and drink available nearby, also welcomes visitors.

Inland Sea
Lago Enriquillo is believed to have been linked to the bay of Port-au-Prince and the sea until tectonic shifts in the earth's surface about one million years ago closed this access and turned it into a lake. This explains both the saltiness and the presence of seashells and coral fragments.

 There are no recommended restaurants in La Descubierta, but a number of stalls sell street food around Las Barias Balneario

27

Left **Columbus's House, La Isabela Bay** Right **Sir Francis Drake greeting a local chief**

Moments in History

1 c.500 BC: Taino Culture
The Taino people arrive on the island they call Quisqueya after a centuries-long canoe-borne migration up the Caribbean archipelago from the Orinoco Delta in South America. A peaceful village-based society of fishermen and farmers, they worship gods of nature and the afterlife.

2 1492: Columbus Arrives
The Genoese explorer sets foot on Quisqueya, which he believes to be near China, and renames it Hispaniola. The discovery heralds the advent of Spanish colonialism as well as the rapid extermination of the Tainos. The city of Santo Domingo is founded in 1498.

3 1586: Francis Drake Sacks Santo Domingo
The golden age of the Spanish colony ends when the English privateer loots and vandalizes his way through its main town. By now, English, French, and Dutch pirates are a constant threat to Hispaniola and other Spanish colonies (see p9).

4 1697: Treaty of Ryswick
After many years of growing French presence in the west of the island, an agreement divides Hispaniola between French Saint Domingue and Spanish

Santo Domingo. The French create a huge prosperous colony, based on slavery and sugar, while the underpopulated Spanish side languishes, dominated by large ranches and the Church.

5 1804: Haitian Independence
Following 13 years of revolution and civil war, an army of former slaves drives out Napoleon's troops from Saint Domingue, declaring Haitian independence. The Spanish colony is invaded and reinvaded, but is returned to Spanish rule in 1809. Several Haitian invasions end with the occupation of Spanish Santo Domingo in February 1822.

6 1844: Independence
Led by Juan Pablo Duarte, a group of nationalists stage a revolt against the 22-year-old Haitian occupation, declaring a separate, independent Dominican Republic. The Haitians are driven out after wealthy Dominican landowners recruit a peasant army. Duarte is quickly sidelined as regional *caudillos* (strongmen) struggle for political control.

7 1915–25: US Occupation
The Marines land in Santo Domingo to impose peace and "restore order" in a country

Columbus's statue, Parque Colón

Previous pages **Exterior of Catedral Santa María de la Encarnación, Santo Domingo**

Trujillo's casket, Santo Domingo

wracked by infighting. The US presence brings foreign investment in the sugar industry and throws peasants off their land. The occupation also creates a National Police Force, from which emerges the dictator Rafael Leonidas Trujillo, "the Benefactor".

1961: Assassination of Trujillo

Thirty years of brutal dictatorship come to an end when Trujillo is gunned down in Santo Domingo. Trujillo had become enormously rich and all-powerful, imprisoning, exiling, and murdering his opponents. He even had the capital renamed Ciudad Trujillo in his honor. His death signals a gradual move towards democracy.

1970s: Arrival of Tourism

The first steps in creating a tourism industry take place with the building of hotels on the North Coast. Over the next three decades the country shrugs off its reliance on sugar and becomes a major player in Caribbean tourism.

1996: First Fair Elections

A sorry record of voting fraud ends with the country's first free and fair elections. After 30 years of dominating politics, Trujillo's former puppet president, Joaquín Balaguer, is forced to retire at the age of 89, allowing Leonel Fernández to win.

Top 10 Heroes & Villains

1 Christopher Columbus (1451–1506)
Visionary explorer or deluded gold hunter? Opinions remain mixed on the man who started the Spanish colony.

2 Bartolomé de Las Casas (1474–1566)
Courageous priest who protested against the Spanish extermination of the Tainos to the King of Spain.

3 Enriquillo (1498–1535)
Leader of the last Taino revolt against the Spanish.

4 Sir Francis Drake (1540–1596)
Hated in the Spanish world as a Protestant bigot.

5 Jean-Pierre Boyer (1776–1850)
Power-hungry Haitian president who ordered the 1821 invasion, abolishing slavery but imposing a military rule.

6 Juan Pablo Duarte (1813–1876)
The revered father of the Dominican nation; a patriot who freed his country.

7 Ulíses Heureaux (1845–1899)
Dictator (1882–1899), who tried to sell the Germans a naval station in Samaná.

8 Trujillo (1891–1961)
The nastiest dictator of them all ordered the massacre of 15,000 Haitians in 1937.

9 María Montez (1912–1951)
Glamorous Barahona-born actress, who made it big in Hollywood in the 1940s.

10 Joaquín Balaguer (1906–2002)
A politician who didn't like losing, he won six dubious elections from 1966 to 1994.

Left **Taino petroglyphs, Las Caritas** Right **Exhibits from Altos de Chavón Archeological Museum**

🔟 Taino Indian Sites

1 El Pomier Caves
Officially a Reserva Antropológica, this network of 57 bat-infested caves north of San Cristóbal contains the largest display of Taino wall paintings and rock drawings in the Caribbean. You can see mysterious spiritual symbols and scenes of day-to-day pre-Columbian life depicted here. ✦ Map D4 • La Toma, San Cristóbal • Open 8am–5pm daily

2 Las Caritas
The "little faces" chiseled into the coral rock of the cave overlooking Lago Enriquillo have a range of expressions. Local legend has it that the renegade Taino leader Enriquillo (see p31) hid in this cave while on the run from the Spanish. ✦ Map A4 • La Descubierta, Lake Enriquillo

Cave entrance, Parque Nacional del Este

3 Cueva El Puente
This long cave holding almost 70 figurative and abstract petroglyphs is in the northeastern section of the Parque Nacional del Este (see p41). Permission and a guide are available from the booth located at the main parking area in central Bayahibe. ✦ Map H5

4 Cueva de Panchito
Food and ceramic remains found in this cave in the Parque Nacional del Este indicate that it was actively used by the Tainos. A carving of a great zemi appears on the wall, along with about 30 other petroglyphs. Permission and an official guide are available in Bayahibe. ✦ Map G5

5 Altos de Chavón Archeological Museum
Located near the shores of the Chavón river, tucked behind the Church of St. Stanislaus, this museum holds more than 3,000 Taino artifacts. The powerful spiritual dimension of Taino society is vividly brought to life by the exhibits on display. ✦ Map G4 • Altos de Chavón • Open 9am–8pm Tue–Sun

6 Cueva de las Maravillas
This complex of grottoes and labyrinths exhibits not only Taino art forms but also stalactites, stalagmites, and other geological curiosities. The 472 pictographs and 19 petroglyphs depict human figures and various animals associated with death rituals. ✦ Map F4 • 809 390 8180 • Open 9am–5pm Tue–Sun • Adm

7 Los Indios de Chacuey
An indigenous (and much smaller) version of Stonehenge, in England, a circle of rocks surrounds a stone slab in the middle of a huge open space. Nearby, religious petroglyphs

Taino village, La Isabela

suggest that this was an important ceremonial center. Look for a local guide in one of the nearby villages. ◈ *Map A2*

La Isabela
The museum at the Parque Nacional Histórico La Isabela *(see p18)* highlights the everyday life in a Taino village. Outside you can still see traces of the foundations of the original settlement as well as an example of an indigenous *bohío* or thatched dwelling, and gardens containing staple crops grown by Taino communities. ◈ *Map C1*

Parque Nacional Los Haitises
Inhospitable mangrove swamps and rocky terrain mean that the Taino sites can best be accessed through an organized boat trip from Sabana de la Mar, Sánchez or Samaná. Caves within the park have extensive drawings, including scenes of hunting, birds, whales, and various faces. ◈ *Map E3*

Cueva de Berna
This is one of the most spectacular caves in the Parque Nacional del Este, and the only one that has been scientifically excavated. More than 300 petroglyphs are distributed along the walls. ◈ *Map H4 • Boca de Yuma • Open 8am–2pm daily*

Top 10 Taino Legacies

Barbecue
The Tainos liked to cook their meat and fish over *barbacoas*, outdoor charcoal-fueled grills.

Bohío
A rectangular house of wooden walls and thatched roof, widely seen in rural areas and villages.

Canoe
One of many Taino words *(canoa)* and inventions still in use today.

Cassava
A mainstay of the pre-Columbian diet, this is made from *manioc*, a root that is poisonous unless properly prepared into flour.

Hammock
The Taino *hamaca* was the favored sleeping arrangement, raising its occupants above rats and other pests.

Hurricane
Huracán was an awe-inspiring god, symbolizing the terrifying power and violence of the natural world.

Petroglyphs
The carvings of human faces, animals, and abstract forms scratched onto rock, often in caves.

Pictographs
Drawings, usually made with charcoal against a pale rockface, showing everyday and spiritual imagery.

Tobacco
The Tainos smoked the leaves of *tabaco* only in their ceremonies.

Zemis
Idols or fetishes representing the many spirits, ancestral and natural, which the Tainos devoutly and religiously worshiped.

Dominican Republic's Top 10

33

Left **Exhibit, Museo de Arte Moderno** Right **Mask, Museo del Hombre Dominicano**

Museums

1 Museo del Hombre Dominicano

Perhaps the country's best museum, its collection of pre-Columbian artifacts reveals the intricacy of indigenous sculpture in the shape of jewelry and religious figurines or *zemis*. Another display charts the impact of African slavery on culture with an eye-opening exhibition of carnival costumes and a model of a voodoo altar *(see p11)*.
✪ *Map L3 • Plaza de Cultura, Santo Domingo • Open 10am–5pm Tue–Sun • Adm*

2 Museo de las Casas Reales

Banner, Museo del Hombre Dominicano

The colonial period is highlighted in this museum, housed in the 16th-century governor's Supreme Court. Period paintings and furniture give a powerful taste of the luxurious lifestyle of the Spanish élite, while a collection of weapons shows how the Tanios were subjugated.
✪ *Map P5 • Calle Las Damas, Zona Colonial, Santo Domingo • 809 682 4202 • Open 9am–5pm Tue–Sun • Adm*

3 Museo Juan Pablo Duarte

Freedom fighter Pablo Duarte *(see p31)* is honored in this modest one-story house where he was born. The mementos mostly comprise documents and paintings, but the three elegant rooms also contain fine furniture and iconography relating to Duarte's underground independence organization, La Trinitaria. ✪ *Map P5 • 308 Calle Isabel la Católica, Santo Domingo • 809 687 1436 • Open 9am–4pm Mon–Sat • Adm*

4 Museo de las Hermanas Mirabal

The small town of Salcedo is unexceptional, apart from its museum commemorating the lives and deaths of the three Mirabal sisters, courageous opponents of Trujillo, who were murdered on the orders of the dictator in 1960. The little family house contains a collection of photographs and every-day personal effects.
✪ *Map D2 • Carretera Salcedo–Tenares, Secc. Conuco, Salcedo • 809 587 8530 • Open 9:30am–5pm Tue–Sat • Adm*

5 Centro Léon

This museum showcases an excellent collection of Dominican art as well as anthropological items such as a reconstructed Taino grave and an exhibition about ecology and biodiversity.
✪ *Map C2 • Av 27 de Febrero 146, Santiago • 809 582 2315 • Open 10am–7pm Tue–Sun • Adm • www.centroleon.org.do*

6 Museo de la Familia Dominicana del Siglo XIX

The house in which this 19th-century collection of domestic items is kept is more interesting than the museum itself. The 1503

Santo Domingo (see map, right), is home to the country's most impressive museums

mansion contains the only double Gothic window in the Americas. This colonial gem also exhibits the furniture and personal effects of a well-to-do Santo Domingo family. ⊗ Map P6
• Casa de Tostado, Calle Arzobispo Meriño 60, Santo Domingo • 809 689 5000 • Open 9:30am–4:30pm Tue–Sun • Adm

Museo de Arte Moderno
The four-story modern art gallery demonstrates the vitality and range of contemporary Dominican creativity. Permanent exhibitions are interspersed with temporary shows, including bucolic paintings of idealized rural life and darker, more sinister meditations on poverty and the country's violent past.
⊗ Map L3 • Plaza de la Cultura, Santo Domingo • 809 685 2153 • Open 10am–6pm Tue–Sun • Adm

Museo Bellapart
This museum is a surprising oasis of fine art within an uptown car showroom. The private collection here encompasses big names of modern Dominican art such as Jaime Colson, the master of rustic realism, and the Spanish anarchist exile José Vela Zanetti, whose impressionistic celebration of peasant life forms the centerpiece of the gallery. ⊗ Map K2
• Corner Av John F Kennedy & Lambert Peguero, Santo Domingo
• Open 9am–6pm Mon–Fri, 9am–12:30pm Sat

Museo de la Comunidad Judía de Sosúa
The small exhibition next door to Sosúa's synagogue tells the

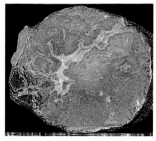

Larimar, Museo de Larimar

story of the country's Jewish community, invited by Trujillo in 1940 to form an agricultural colony. Photographs, letters, and 1940s artifacts explain how they fled the Nazis, settled in this North Coast town, and started a dairy cooperative. ⊗ Map D1
• Calle Dr Alejo Martínez, Sosúa • Open 9am–noon & 2–4pm Mon–Fri, 9am–noon Sat • Adm

Museo de Larimar
This multilingual exhibition explains the process of mining and shaping larimar, a semi-precious blue stone mined solely in the Dominican Republic, into jewelry. It's situated in a lovely colonial-period house, where on the ground floor you can buy fine examples of larimar jewels. ⊗ Map P5 • 54 Calle Isabel la Católica, Santo Domingo
• Open 10am–5:45pm daily

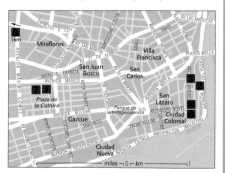

Left **Horse-drawn carriages, Malecón** Center **Monkey Jungle** Right **Ocean World**

⑩ Children's Activities

1 Acuario Nacional, Santo Domingo

Flanking the Caribbean Sea, the aquarium features a large plastic tunnel in which spectators are surrounded by water, sharks, rays, and conger eels. Colorful shoals of fish swarm around the tunnel, while other exhibits throughout the aquarium explain different sorts of marine environments. ⊛ *Map E4 • Av España 75 • 809 766 1709 • Open 9:30am–5:30pm Tue–Sun • Adm*

Acuario Nacional

2 Agua Splash Caribe, Santo Domingo

This theme park has everything for swimmers and water-lovers, including 12 slides and pools of varying depth. There is ample shade, and refreshments are available. Weekends are very popular with local families. ⊛ *Map E4 • Av España 50 • 809 766 1927 • Open Jun–Aug: 11am–7pm Tue–Sun; Sep–May: 11am–6pm Thu–Sun • Adm*

3 Parque Zoológico Nacional, Santo Domingo

An expansive 400-acre (162 ha) park of tropical gardens and water features, the zoo is home to tigers as well as more local fauna such as flamingos and the elusive Dominican mammals, *hutías* and *solenodons*. Children will enjoy spotting creatures in sympathetically landscaped compounds as well as riding in the shuttle train. ⊛ *Map E4 • Av Los Arroyos • 809 378 2149 • Open 10am–5:30pm Tue–Sun • Adm*

4 Horse-drawn Carriages

Small horse-drawn carts clip-clop up and down Santo Domingo's scenic Malecón as well as around the atmospheric Zona Colonial. Similarly relaxed and child-friendly sightseeing takes place in Santiago, where the focal point is the central Parque Duarte. Prices for a fixed time should be negotiated before you set off.

5 Fun City Action Park, Puerto Plata

Car-racing fans can come to Fun City's four go-kart runways, where there is ample opportunity for both children and parents to test their driving skills. There's also a separate area provided for smaller children, with bumper cars, slides and see-saws. ⊛ *Map C1 • Carretera Puerto Plata–Sosúa, near Playa Dorada • 809 320 1031 • Open 10am–6pm Mon–Fri, 10am–8pm Sat & Sun • Adm • www.funcity-gokarts.com*

6 Ocean World, Puerto Plata

This marine theme park offers interactive experiences such as swimming with bottle-nose dolphins, exploring an imitation reef, feeding sea lions, and getting close to sharks. There are many exhibits, a gift shop, and a restaurant. Environmentalists are critical of the concept of keeping dolphins in captivity. ◈ Map C1 • Playa Cofresí • 809 291 1000 • Open 9am–6pm daily • Adm

7 Dolphin World, Cabeza de Toro, Punta Cana

With dolphin swims that can be enjoyed by children aged one and over (with an adult) and catamaran coastal cruises taking in the reef Sanctuary Cabeza de Toro and beautiful beaches, there is something for everyone at this conservation-focused marine animal park (see p23). ◈ Map H4 • 809 468 2000 • www.dolphinexplorer.com.do

8 Monkey Jungle, Sosúa

Free-roaming, tame monkeys make this botanical garden a hit with all children. There is also an exciting zipline adventure for children aged over two. ◈ Map D1 • 829 649 4555 • Open 9am–4pm daily • www.monkeyjungledr.com

Horseback Riding, at El Limon

9 Horseback Riding

Almost every all-inclusive beach resort will either offer or be able to recommend horseback riding facilities. The small, normally patient Dominican horses are a good way to introduce kids to riding, especially on soft sand. More ambitious excursions in mountain terrain are available for experienced riders through specialist companies (see p42).

10 Baseball

Older children may enjoy the buzz of an evening baseball game, especially if familiar with the rules. The floodlit spectacle is usually accompanied by lots of music and razzmatazz as well as snacks galore. Children are welcome, though the game may end rather too late for younger ones (see p38).

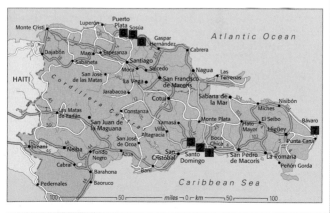

Left **Baseball at Parque Mirador del Sur** Right **Locals fishing**

TOP 10 Sports & Activities

1 Baseball
You can watch the local kids play, or have a go yourself at any local park, but to experience the fanaticism with which Dominicans follow baseball, you should visit one of the top grounds – Estadio Tetelo Vargas, San Pedro de Macorís *(see p72)* or La Romana *(see pp24–5)*.

2 Golf
The Dominican Republic is home to several top golf courses, two of which are located to the east of Punta Cana – Cap Cana, designed by Jack Nicklaus, and Casa de Campo. In the north, other prominent golf sites include Playa Grande and Playa Dorada – both designed by Robert Trent Jones, and Los Marlins and Guavaberry in Juan Dolio.

3 Tennis
You'll find tennis courts at all major hotels, and it's usually possible to hire rackets on site. The biggest complex is at Casa de Campo where professionals advise you on the game.

Golf course in Punta Cana Beach Resort

4 Basketball
Second to baseball in most Dominicans' affections, and growing all the time, this sport is played in every town and village by the locals, and there's nothing to stop visitors taking part. The main venue for serious games is Santo Domingo's Centro Olímpico, where the would-be professionals display their skills.

5 Cycling
Although cycling isn't safe in most towns and cities, the countryside is full of relatively quiet, if potholed, roads, and there is no shortage of off-road possibilities, especially in the Cordillera Central. Bikes can be hired from specialist tour operators *(see p127)*, who also lead organized excursions.

6 Fishing
Lake and river fishing are popular with locals, but angling-inclined visitors will want to have a go at deep-sea fishing, where sea bass and red snapper are favorites. For those who prefer a Hemingway-style contest, there is big-game fishing for marlin, setting out from Palmar de Océa and Cabeza de Toro *(see p43)*.

7 Horse Racing
Dominicans like to bet, especially on cockfighting, but horses also have their fans, particularly at Santo Domingo's V Centenario racetrack. Here, gambling alternates with drinking.

The professional baseball season runs from November to February

8 Go-karting

With most adults happy to drive their cars at breakneck speed on the country's roads, this is reserved for children, although there's no reason why grown-ups can't roar around the corners. There's an excellent track near Puerto Plata *(see p36)*. ✎ *Fun City Action Park: Map C1; Carretera Puerto Plata–Sosúa; 809 320 1031; open 10am–6pm Mon–Fri, 10am–7pm Sat & Sun*

9 Bowling

Another United States import eagerly embraced by the Dominican youth, bowling has taken off as a popular family activity following the opening of a couple of state-of-the-art venues. The Sebelén Bowling Center in the capital is big and technically impressive, while Punta Cana has its own championship-standard alley. ✎ *Sebelén Bowling Center: Santo Domingo; 809 920 0202; open 3pm–midnight Mon–Thu, 3pm–1am Fri, 10am–1am Sat, noon–midnight Sun • Punta Cana Lanes: Plaza Bolera, Punta Cana, Higüey; open 4pm–midnight Mon–Thu, 4pm–2am Fri, 1pm–2am Sat, 1pm–midnight Sun*

Bowling

10 Polo

Legend has it that polo was introduced in 1954 by the Indian maharaja Jabar Singh, who was hired to teach the dictator Trujillo's sons. Its main home is now the exclusive Casa de Campo resort, where only the seriously rich can play, under the eye of the maharaja's sons. Visitors are also allowed to watch the matches during weekends. ✎ *Casa de Campo: Map G4 • 809 200 1304 • www.casadecampo.com.do*

Top 10 Baseball Players

1 Tetelo Vargas (1906–1971)
Revered in San Pedro de Macorís as a star outfielder and courageous opponent of dictator Rafael Trujillo.

2 'Ozzie' Virgil (b. 1932)
The first Dominican to make it big time in the US Major League in the 1950s.

3 Felipe Alou (b. 1935)
This power hitter enjoyed a long career as a player and award-winning manager.

4 Juan Marichal (b. 1937)
Popularly known as the "Dominican Dandy" for his flamboyant style, Marichal was a record-breaking pitcher.

5 Ricardo Carty (b. 1939)
Carty was so impressive as a youngster that ten clubs tried to sign him up.

6 Tony Peña (b. 1957)
A four-time Golden Glover, he was an adept catcher and then a highly rated manager.

7 Sammy Sosa (b. 1968)
A household name, who rose from shoe shining to become a millionaire star and philanthropist.

8 Pedro Martínez (b. 1971)
Widely considered to be simply the best pitcher in the US Major League.

9 Alex Rodríguez (b. 1975)
Arguably the world's best, Rodríguez is also the youngest player ever to reach 600 home runs.

10 Albert Pujols (b. 1980)
A member of the current generation of Dominican exports, and a rising superstar of powerful batting.

Dominican Republic's Top 10

Left & Center **Waterfall & gorges near Jarabacoa** Right **View of Playa San Rafael**

Nature Trails

Pico Duarte
The biggest challenge of them all, this mountain can be reached from several trails, the most popular setting off from La Ciénaga (see p82). The round trip takes three days on average, and an official guide must accompany walkers. You'll pass through pine forests, meadows, and rocky terrain (see p13). ⬉ Map C3

Jarabacoa
The town provides the perfect base for walking or riding through the lush Dominican Alps (see pp12–13), where waterfalls, clear rivers, and gorges are to be found among meadows and pine forests. There are many trails in the area, varying from gentle strolls through farmland to day-long mountain treks. ⬉ Map C3

Constanza
This idyllic, cool valley is the starting point for many recommended trails, which take you through pine forests and into flower-covered mountain meadows. Bird-watching is a big draw here, with Hispaniolan woodpeckers, parakeets, and hummingbirds in abundance. The trail to the Salto Agua Blanca is manageable and often spectacular (see pp12–13). ⬉ Map C3

Parque Nacional Monte Cristi
Most of this sprawling wilderness comprises desert and hard-to-reach mangrove swamps. But the large humpback mountain of El Morro is easily accessible from the park office, offering a great walk through a cutting onto the beach. This is the place to appreciate the Northwest's ecosystem (see p95). ⬉ Map A1
• Open daily • Adm

Pico Isabel de Torres
If you don't want to take the cable car to the top of the mountain, you can always choose the 4-hour hike up a steep rainforest-clad slope. Guides are

El Morro, Parque Nacional Monte Cristi

Parque Nacional del Este

recommended, as it's easy to stray off the paths and get lost. The lush vegetation is home to parakeets and many other birds *(see pp17 & 47)*. ◎ *Map C1*

6 Los Haïtises, Sabana de la Mar

The isolated sandy bays and caves here were formerly used by pirates. You need a guide to enter the protected area; the jungle trail from Caño Hondo to Caño Salado leads to caves containing Taíno pictographs.
◎ *Map F3 • Oficina de Parque Nacional Los Haïtises, Paseo el Lupina Cordero 5, Sabana de la Mar • Open 8am–6pm daily • Adm*

7 Parque Nacional del Este

This large area of wilderness contains dry tropical forest, mangroves and the Robinson Crusoe Island of Saona. An official

guide must be hired, and a boat trip from Bayahibe is the best way to reach the otherwise inaccessible nature trails *(see p73)*. ◎ *Map G5 • Adm*

8 Baní Dunes

The extensive dunes on the Las Salinas peninsula *(see p109)* are one of the country's best-kept secrets. An expanse of sandy hummocks, dotted with sea grape and marine grasses, rolls down to the glittering Caribbean. ◎ *Map D5*

9 San Rafael

Inland from the deservedly popular beach and swimming hole, the river that fills the pool flows and falls down a hillside covered with boulders, ferns, and tropical trees. A hike up the riverside path passes a series of small waterfalls and leads to magnificent sea views. ◎ *Map B5*

10 Parque Nacional Baoruco

Baoruco boasts the greatest variety of landscapes and flora, ranging from dust-dry, low-level hillsides to exuberantly tropical rainforests. A four-wheel-drive is essential to reach the wild orchids and pine forest. ◎ *Map A5*

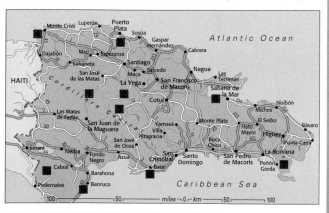

Left **Playa Dorada** Center **Windsurfing at Bávaro Resort** Right **Starfish, Parque Nacional del Este**

ᴛᴏᴘ10 Beach & Sea Activities

1 Swimming
There are good swimming options all around the country, but as a general rule the beaches on the South Caribbean coast have calmer waters than those on the Atlantic north. While some resort beaches have lifeguards, most public ones do not, so be cautious of strong currents.

2 Windsurfing
The placid waters of the South Coast are probably the best bet for novices, but Cabarete, with its powerful tides, is a magnet for true aficionados, drawing world-class competitors to the annual World Cup Wind-surfing Competition in June. Equipment can be hired from most seaside hotels. You may also get your training lessons at the Kiteclub Cabarete. Ⓢ *Kiteclub Cabarete: Map C3 • 809 571 9748 • www. kiteclubcabarete.com*

3 Kitesurfing
Also centered around the surging surf beaches of the Cabarete area, this sport is growing in popularity because the use of a huge kite to produce momentum requires less wind than does a windsurfer's sail. With a following breeze, good kitesurfers can make huge leaps. Ⓢ *Vela Cabarete: Map D1 • 809 571 0805 • www. velacabarete.com*

4 Standup Paddle Boarding
Rent a board and go on a 'surfari'! This fun experience is an eco-friendly addition to the watersports available on the island. Ⓢ *809 609 4045 • www. bayahibesup.com*

5 Scuba Diving
Most dive companies are owned by Europeans or North Americans, who offer training as well as rental equipment. Diving around the country is incredibly varied, yielding up 16th-century shipwrecks, coral reefs, and marine life. Try the Northern Coast Diving in Sosúa or Diving Dominican Republic in Bayahibe. Ⓢ *Northern Coast Diving, Sosúa: Map D1; 809 571 1028; www.northerncoastdiving.com • Diving Dominican Republic, Bayahibe: Map G4; 829 341 9185; www.divingdr.com*

Horse riding

6 Horseback Riding
The country's beautiful beaches are ideal for horseback riding against a scenic background of sea and coconut trees. Hotels and tour operators can make arrangements. Ⓢ *Sea Horse Ranch: Map D1 • near Sosúa • 809 571 4462*

7 Cavern Diving
The country's rugged limestone terrain is riddled with underwater caves and canyons which can be explored

For more information on Sea Horse Ranch log on to www.sea-horse-ranch.com

by experienced divers. You can swim through some tunnels, and examine the huge sponges and other sea creatures that live in the half-light of this submarine world. Golden Arrows Dive Center can plan your diving tours. ✪ *Golden Arrows Dive Center: Map E4 • 809 566 7780 or 809 886 7777 • www.cavediving.com.do*

8 Deep Sea and Sport Fishing

Experience the joy of deep sea and sport fishing under the guidance of some of the country's top captains and fishermen. Crewed catamarans are also available for hire at the Cap Cana Marina. ✪ *Map H4 • www.mikesmarina.info*

Sail boats, Luperón

9 Sail Boats

Boats and catamarans are available at the main tourist resorts in the country. A good option is the small Hobie One cat (boats), to be found as part of all-inclusive packages at places such as Bávaro, Boca Chica *(see p71)*, Puerto Plata, Punta Cana, and Bayahibe.

10 Snorkeling

A snorkel and mask allows you to enter a multicolored underwater world of rocks, reefs, and teeming fish. The beaches around Las Terrenas are recommended as a good base for snorkeling.

Top 10 Activity Beaches

1 Cabarete
The best-known and sometimes busiest beach for all sorts of surfing. ✪ *Map D1*

2 Las Salinas
Another firm favorite with surfers, a yellow-sand beach set among saltpans and rolling dunes. ✪ *Map D5*

3 Playa Punta Cana
This long strip of soft sand offers plenty of scope for kayaking, sailing, and snorkeling. ✪ *Map H4*

4 Playa Bávaro
Another well-equipped stretch of beach, where independent dive operators compete with the all-inclusive amenities. ✪ *Map H4*

5 Playa Dorada
A beach of pristine sand, ideal for paragliding and building sandcastles. ✪ *Map C1*

6 El Portillo
Home of the Samaná Peninsula's biggest all-inclusive, this popular beach features every possible sporting activity. ✪ *Map F2*

7 Sosúa
A protected crescent cove in the town's center with an easily accessible reef that attracts snorkelers. ✪ *Map D1*

8 Playa Dominicus
Surrounded by all-inclusive resorts, this safe beach offers windsurfing, diving, snorkeling, and kayaking. ✪ *Map G4*

9 Las Terrenas
Many activities are available, including swimming and snorkeling. ✪ *Map F2*

10 Boca Chica
Packed at weekends, the gently sloping beach is ideal for undemanding snorkeling and swimming. ✪ *Map F4*

Left **Playa Isabela** Right **Playa Rincón**

TOP 10 Quiet Beaches

1 Playa del Morro
A rocky track cuts through a gap in the landmark mountain of El Morro, leading to a deserted white-sand beach. The beach is walled in by sheer cliffs, but the water is calm and protected in this spectacular cove. Sunsets are superb. ✎ Map A1

2 Playa Isabela
Steeped in history as the site of the first European settlement in the Americas, this low-key stretch of sand backed by shade-giving vegetation attracts more fishermen than tourists. The freshwater Bajabonico River meets the sea at this spot, producing an interesting ecosystem that's worth exploring. ✎ Map B1

3 Playa Bonita
This is probably the nearest thing to the classic image of tropical paradise. White sand meets calm turquoise sea,

Boats, Playa Isabela

watched over by a stretch of coconut palms. Even the nearby hotels and guesthouses fail to intrude on the peaceful beach heaven *(see p21)*. ✎ Map F2

4 Playa Rincón
Lack of easy access due to a single connecting rough road, has kept this beautiful horseshoe cove free from obtrusive development. The sand is pristinely white, the sea bluer than blue, and the coconut trees sway enticingly *(see p102)*. ✎ Map F2

5 Playa Limón
A beach for exploring rather than swimming. A long, wild, deserted 6-mile (10-km) stretch, where big breakers crash onto the palm-littered sand. As part of a protected National Park, the beach has escaped development and offers nature in the wild, including mangroves, coconut groves, and hungry mosquitoes. ✎ Map G3

6 Playa Macao
Only a few miles from the well-tended beaches of Bávaro and Punta Cana, this long, sweeping stretch of untamed coastline is as undeveloped as anywhere in the country. Pounding surf and a powerful undertow discourage most swimmers, but the bay at Punta Macao, with its sheltering headlands, is safer. ✎ Map H3

7 Playa Corbanito

The white sand may not be the finest in the Dominican Republic, but the view over the Bahía de Ocoa towards the distant sierra is breathtaking. The bay's water is calm and inviting, and the beach itself, untroubled by tourists and home only to a few fishermen, is attractive and extremely relaxing. ◈ Map C5

Playa Cabo Rojo

8 Playa Baoruco

Harboring one of the many small and undeveloped beaches on the coastline south of Barahona (see p110), Baoruco is more a fishing village than a tourist resort but it has a small luxury hotel, Casa Bonita, with a great view (see p132). The pretty beach has white pebbles, and the views into the wooded mountains are stunning. ◈ Map B5

9 Playa Cabo Rojo

Lying on the coastline of Parque Nacional Jaragua (see p111), this "Red Cape" is named for the rich red seams of bauxite that once fed a now-derelict processing plant. The wilderness is certainly a draw for the pelicans and other birds. ◈ Map A6

10 Bahia de las Aguilas

One of the most beautiful and unspoilt beaches in the country, the pristine Bahia de las Aguilas is also the hardest to reach. Fishing boats from the village, Las Cuevas, transport visitors to and from the beach; a return trip costs US$45. Facilities here are minimal, so carry water and other necessities. ◈ Map A6

A resort near Baoruco Beach

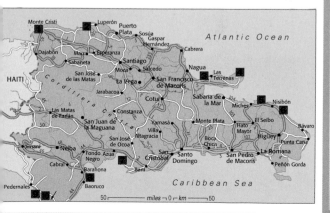

Left **Santo Cerro** Right **View from the San Felipe Fortress, Puerto Plata**

📖10 Views

1 Torre del Homenaje, Santo Domingo

After a challenging climb up a spiral staircase, look out over the mouth of the Ozama River and across the water at the looming Columbus Lighthouse. Best of all is the panoramic view of the Zona Colonial, a grid of low-level whitewashed buildings nestling amid lush tropical trees. 🔗 Map P5
• Calle Las Damas • Open 9am–4pm Mon–Sat, 10am–4pm Sun • Adm

2 Carretera 12

The winding but well-maintained road leading up from Bonao (see p80) to the Constanza Valley is one of the country's most fabulous. It meanders through pine forests and over rushing streams. As the temperature drops, there are superb views of the mountain range and the valley. 🔗 Map C3

3 Santo Cerro

The site of a Spanish victory over the Tainos and a holy pilgrimage place, this mountain-top church is surrounded by a belvedere from where views extend for miles over the fertile Cibao Valley. The forested mountains and green valley floor might look European were it not for the palm trees (see p81). 🔗 Map D2

4 Pico Duarte

This peak offers excellent views, though only the toughest and most experienced hikers can undertake the expedition to the top of the Caribbean's highest mountain. On a clear day, the Caribbean Sea can be seen to the south and huge Lago Enriquillo to the west (see pp13 & 40). 🔗 Map C3

5 Monumento a los Héroes, Santiago

Trujillo's monument may not be to everyone's taste, but a climb to the top of the tower is rewarded by a wonderful view over the surprisingly large city and the surrounding countryside (see pp15 & 52). 🔗 Map C2

View of Ozam River from Torre del Homanaje

6 San Felipe Fortress, Puerto Plata

Standing on the battlements of this ancient bastion situated on a promontory, behold the Atlantic, over the calm Puerto Plata Bay, or the majestic Pico Isabel de Torres *(see p17)*. Late afternoons are spectacular, as the mountain changes color with the setting sun *(see p16)*. ⊗ *Map C1*

7 Pico Isabel de Torres, Puerto Plata

Watched over by a 54-ft (16-m) statue of Christ, the long Atlantic coastline stretches to the horizon. Hotel clusters and other modern developments line the white beaches. The town of Puerto Plata *(see pp16–17)* lies beneath, the cathedral clearly visible, and inland the mountains of the Cordillera Septentrional. It is best to visit in the morning as visibility deteriorates in the afternoon. ⊗ *Map C1*

8 Naranjita

The serpentine road linking the beach resort of Las Terrenas *(see pp20–21 & 102)* to the town of Sánchez, although in poor condition, works its way over the spine of the peninsula, reaching

View of Río Chavón from Altos de Chavón

1,312 ft (400 m) near Naranjita village. From the roadside you can take in enormous vistas of coconut trees, offshore islands, and the coastline ahead. ⊗ *Map F2*
• *Samaná Peninsula*

9 Altos de Chavón

This mock Tuscan village stands on a bluff commanding wonderful views of the Chavón River, as it flows gently through a wooded ravine bordered by coconut trees *(see p25)*. ⊗ *Map G4*

10 Corbanito

A long, gray-sand beach backed by a few fishermen's huts and palm trees faces the Bahía de Ocoa, a calm inlet of glittering water ringed by mountains. The view across the bay is a mix of distant hillsides and sky, while the Sierra El Número mountain rises behind. ⊗ *Map D5*

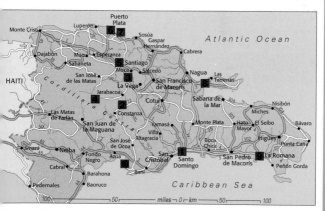

Left & Center **Catedral Santa María de la Encarnación** Right **Catedral de Santiago Apóstol**

🔟 Places of Worship

1 Capilla de la Virgen del Rosario, Santo Domingo

Marooned on the industrial eastern side of the Ozama River, this tiny chapel is a reminder of the country's original capital. The existing church is a white-washed structure, with three brick portals, and dates from the 19th century, but the first wooden chapel was built in 1498. ◈ *Map P3 • Av Olegario Vargas • Open 10:30am–4pm daily*

2 Catedral Santa María de la Encarnación, Santo Domingo

The oldest cathedral in the Americas, this building is a treasure-trove of Gothic, Baroque, and Renaissance styles, with a mahogany altar, elaborate friezes and sculptures, and stained-glass windows. There are 14 separate chapels inside, one of which housed the remains of Columbus until 1992, when they were moved to the Columbus Lighthouse. ◈ *Map P5 • Parque Colón • Open 9am–4pm daily*

3 Santa Bárbara, Santo Domingo

The uncertain nature of colonial life is reflected by this church-cum-fort, dedicated to the patron saint of soldiers and explosives. The church was vandalized by Sir Francis Drake's pirates in 1586, and later damaged by a hurricane. ◈ *Map P4 • Calle Isabela la Católica • Open 9am–4pm daily*

4 Iglesia Nuestra Señora de la Consolación, San Cristóbal

The massive mustard-colored parish church, with an imposing tree-lined plaza in front, was built in 1949 at huge public cost by the dictator Trujillo, who was originally buried here. Visitors can see his empty tomb. ◈ *Map D4 • Parque Piedra Viva • Open 8am–5pm daily*

5 Catedral de Santiago Apóstol, Santiago

Look out for the fine carvings on the 1895 cathedral's mahogany doors, showing biblical scenes associated with St. James. Although it's often closed, the three-aisled interior is worth a visit for the marble tomb of Ulíses Heureaux *(see p31)*, and its modern windows by contemporary artist Rincón Mora. ◈ *Map C2 • Parque Duarte • Open 8am–6pm daily*

6 Catedral San Felipe, Puerto Plata

A symmetrical blend of old and new, this cathedral dominates the historic center of town, with its two whitewashed, reinforced-concrete towers visible from afar *(see p17)*. ◈ *Map C1 • Calle Duarte • Open 9am–6pm daily*

Detail on the door Catedral San Felipe

7 Synagogue, Sosúa

A poignant reminder of the Jewish community that fled Nazi Germany to start a colony here, this modest one-room

Women must keep their shoulders covered and men must wear long slacks in all churches and cathedrals

Catedral San Pedro Apóstol

synagogue, with its distinctive Star of David motifs, is housed in a simple but attractive wooden building. ◈ *Map D1 • Calle Martínez • By appointment*

8 La Churcha, Samaná

This red-roofed Non-Conformist church is made of prefabricated parts, sent from England by Methodists in 1823 to cater for English-speaking former slaves from North America who settled here under Haitian rule. ◈ *Map F2 • Calle Teodora Chassereaux • Open 8:30am–noon Sun*

9 Basílica de Nuestra Señora de la Altagracia, Higüey

The Republic's biggest church was designed in the 1950s to replace the smaller original as the site of the annual January 21 pilgrimage in honor of the Virgin of Altagracia, the nation's patron saint *(see p50)*. ◈ *Map G4 • La Altagracia • Open 5am–7pm daily*

10 Catedral San Pedro Apóstol, San Pedro de Macorís

This landmark church, with its all turreted bell-tower features a Romanesque doorway, Gothic-style gargoyles, and an imitation rose window. Rebuilt in 1911, it has long-standing associations with the English-speaking *cocolos*. ◈ *Map F4 • Av Independencia & Av Charro • Open 8am–8pm daily*

Top 10 Religious Buildings in the Zona Colonial

1 Casa de los Jesuitas (1508)
The building, with a fine courtyard, housed a Jesuit-run school of rhetoric. ◈ *Map P5*

2 Monasterio de San Francisco (1508)
The ruins of the New World's first monastery are also used for events. ◈ *Map N5*

3 Hospital San Nicolás de Barí (1503)
The Americas' first hospital, now in ruins, was built in the shape of a cross. ◈ *Map N5*

4 Iglesia de la Altagracia (1922)
This Victorian church is famous for its miracle cures. ◈ *Map N5*

5 Iglesia Santa Clara (1552)
The first Franciscan nunnery in the Americas. ◈ *Map P6*

6 Convento de los Dominicos (1510)
This building became the first university in the Americas in 1538. ◈ *Map N6*

7 Iglesia Regina Angelorum (1537)
This forbidding structure's most impressive feature is its rich Baroque altar. ◈ *Map N6*

8 Iglesia San Lázaro (1650)
This church-hospital specialized in caring for lepers. ◈ *Map N5*

9 Iglesia Nuestra Señora del Carmen (1590)
Duarte's secret Trinitaria organization met here to plot the fight for independence. ◈ *Map N6*

10 Iglesia de Nuestra Señora de las Mercedes (1555)
The church has a distinctive mahogany pulpit. ◈ *Map N5*

→ *Cocolos migrated here from the British Caribbean in the late 19th century*

Left **Carnival masks, La Vega** Right **Parade on Independence Day**

🔟 Festivals & Holidays

1 New Year's Day
Dominicans welcome the New Year with an exuberant open-air concert at different locations in Santo Domingo, at which some of the country's top bands perform. Other towns and villages hold smaller-scale but equally loud outdoor fiestas.

2 Three Kings' Day
The big present-giving day is a crucial part of the extended Christmas–New Year holiday season. In San Pedro de Macorís, some of the town's millionaire baseball stars traditionally hand out bats, balls, and gloves to kids. 🛇 *Jan 6*

3 Virgen de Altagracia
The annual pilgrimage to the modern concrete basilica of Higüey brings thousands of Dominicans together in prayer to the nation's patron saint, followed by a long party. Services and vigils are held across the country, but the Higüey gathering is the most impressive expression of an African-influenced Catholic faith. 🛇 *Jan 21*

4 Carnival
Every Dominican village, town, and city organizes some sort of event every Sunday in

Devil costume, Carnival

February. La Vega *(see p81)* is famous for its devil-like Carnival masks, while the northern city of Monte Cristi *(see p95)* witnesses boisterous street battles. The Carnival period reaches an ear-splitting climax in Santo Domingo with a parade of costumes and bands along the Malecón. 🛇 *Sundays in Feb*

5 Independence Day
This marks the anniversary of the country's independence from Haitian occupation on 27 February 1844. It is celebrated with a military parade along the Malecón. 🛇 *Feb 27*

6 Holy Week
Semana Santa is the year's most important religious period, and all activity grinds to a halt as Dominicans go to church or parties, or both. The Catholic celebrations are paralleled by the Haitian community's African-influenced *gagá* ceremonies, which take place near the border and in sugar plantations. 🛇 *Mid-Apr*

7 Merengue Festival
The latter part of the month witnesses a spectacular showcase of Dominican musical talent, as the seafront Malecón in Santo Domingo hosts a series of concerts. 🛇 *July*

8 Restoration Day

The grandiose Monumento a los Héroes de la Restauración *(see p15)* is the scene of a huge party to commemorate the country's "second independence" from Spain in 1865 after a guerrilla struggle that started in Santiago *(see pp14 & 81)*. Another celebration, with plenty of music, takes place in Santo Domingo's beautiful Plaza España. ◐ *Aug 16*

9 Merengue Festival

In the third week in September, the northern port of Puerto Plata hosts a weeklong celebration of merengue talent. Most of the action takes place on the long and normally quiet Malecón, but at this time of year the place comes to life, with bands performing and countless outdoor bars. ◐ *Sep*

10 All Saints

Both Catholics and followers of *vodu* celebrate the Day of the Dead, when, as elsewhere in Latin America and the Caribbean, families visit cemeteries to commune with the deceased, and take small offerings such as flowers and food. This ritual is taken most seriously in the areas near the Haitian border. ◐ *Nov 1*

All Saints celebrations: Day of the Dead

Top 10 Local Festivals

1 Azua (Mar 19)
A big patriotic celebration commemorating a historic Dominican victory over Haitian forces in 1844.

2 Puerto Plata (May 3)
The northern town noisily celebrates San Felipe, the votive day of its local saint.

3 Monte Cristi (May 30)
Fernando Rey festivities are in honor of the 16th-century Spanish monarch, turned into local patron saint.

4 San Juan de la Maguana (June 17–24)
San Juan Bautista, or Saint John the Baptist, is revered in this folkloric religious festival.

5 San Pedro de Macorís (June 29)
The city celebrates its patron saint, San Pedro Apóstol, with lots of music and dance.

6 Santiago (July 24–26)
Santiago Apostól, or Saint James the scourge of the Moors, is the object of great veneration.

7 Higüey (Aug 14)
The cowboy country lets its hair down with a rustic Festival of the Bulls.

8 Baní (Nov 21)
Images of Nuestra Señora de Regla, the town's adopted saint, are carried through the streets in celebration.

9 Boca Chica (Nov 30)
San Andrés or Saint Andrew has his lively *fiesta patronal* in the South Coast tourist town.

10 Samaná (Dec 4)
Santa Bárbara's day is the pretext for processions and partying in Santa Bárbara de Samaná *(see p101)*. The local popular music *bamboula* is played.

Left **Monumento a los Héroes** Center & Right **Tourists & locals at Boca Chica Beach**

10 Places to Meet the Locals

1 Parque Central

Every Dominican town has its own central plaza, shaded by trees, equipped with benches, and often filled with locals. This is the place for people-watching, especially in the early evening, when most of them stroll around. Don't be afraid to smile and say what you can in Spanish.

2 The Malecón

Every evening, the capital's seafront boulevard attracts crowds in search of a cooling breeze. There are open-air bars and other seating areas, and you're bound to strike up a conversation sooner or later. There are some hustlers, but lots of friendly family groups too. At weekends, children come here to fly kites *(see p10)*. ◈ Map M4

Haitian art for sale at the Malecón

3 Calle El Conde

This pedestrian-only shopping strip isn't the prettiest in town, but it's always full of life. Escape the heat and bustle outside by slipping into one of the bars or cafés, and you'll meet plenty of visitors *(see p10)*. ◈ Map N5

4 Parque Mirador del Sur

A large and pleasant expanse of well-tended grass, trees, and tracks, the park is a magnet for joggers, skateboarders, and dog walkers. Younger, health-conscious city dwellers congregate here along with families, especially in the morning and evening, when the through road is shut to cars *(see p11)*. ◈ Map J4

5 Monumento a los Héroes de la Restauración, Santiago

Trujillo's folly is famous for its view, but the large open space around the monument is also a favorite among locals for meeting and having a good time. There are several friendly cafés in the vicinity, but the action gets going at weekends and public holidays *(see pp15 & 46)*.

6 Public Beaches

Locals are often discouraged from using the sand near tourist complexes, so it makes a change to visit a public beach such as Boca Chica or Juan Dolio. Here, Dominican families enjoy themselves in a loud and uninhibited way.

7 Baseball Games

Watching a Dominican baseball game is as much a social as a sporting experience. The crowds are passionate but good-natured and the match is interspersed with a lot of chat, drinking, and snacks. If you're interested in this sport, you'll make new friends *(see p38)*.

8 Carnival

A countrywide affair, the Carnival in February brings out the most gregarious side of the Dominican character, with days of merengue music and rum. Some of the traditional rituals can be rather boisterous, and onlookers may be hit with a pig's bladder, but the emphasis is very much on fun *(see p50)*.

Carnival reveler

9 Colmados

The Dominican institution of the corner-store bar is found in every neighborhood, normally with a well-stocked refrigerator, a television or a steady stream of loud music.

10 Markets

Although they range from big covered halls to a few stalls on a street corner, markets are a crucial part of social life and a great way to meet local people. You might not want to buy much on show, but the atmosphere makes a visit worthwhile.

Shop at Playa Sosúa

Top 10 Customs & Beliefs

1 Politeness
Old-fashioned Hispanic courtesy is important. For example, greeting those present when entering a room.

2 Dress
Even impoverished Dominicans make a huge effort to look well dressed.

3 The Church
Over half of Dominicans claim to be Catholics, even though only a small percentage regularly attend church.

4 Brujería
The Dominican term for magic, black or white, which many people believe in.

5 Botánicas
Stores or market stalls selling religious and superstitious icons and potions for use in *brujería (see above)*.

6 Siestas
Although most offices and shops stay open all day, those outside tourist areas often close for lunch and reopen at 3pm.

7 Hurrying
Almost unknown, and Dominicans do not like pushy foreigners who do not know how to relax.

8 Punctuality
Flexible, especially in social situations. Nevertheless, buses and tours tend to leave on time.

9 Machismo
Totally ingrained among most men, who like to flirt but want their women to stay safely at home.

10 Politics
Presidential and parliamentary elections take place every four years, though most people are skeptical about politicians' promises.

Left **Mercado Modelo** Right **Stalls selling paintings at Cortacito Beach**

🔟 Shopping

1 Mercado Modelo, Santo Domingo

The capital's biggest and most hectic souvenir shopping area is a warren of stalls and booths within a concrete hangar, surrounded by streets crammed with sidewalk vendors. The cornucopia of tourist souvenirs includes Haitian paintings, sculptures, rum, CDs, and exotic items connected with *vodu*. ⊛ *Map N5 • Av Mella 505 • Open 8am–6pm Mon–Sat*

2 Blue Mall

An upscale shopping mall with top brands such as Louis Vuitton, Cartier, and Carolina Herrara. Among the many American chains in the food court are Krispy Kreme and Häagen-Dazs. ⊛ *Map J2 • Av Winston Churchill on corner of Av Gustavo Mejía Ricart*

3 Museo Mundo de Ambar, Santo Domingo

Although there are many amber outlets in the Zona Colonial, this is one of the most reputable,

Tonics for sale outside Mercado Modelo

selling some beautiful examples of jewelry made from the precious resin. Also on sale are earrings and brooches featuring blue and light blue larimar. An exhibition explains the process, and there is sometimes a craftsman at work as well. ⊛ *Map P5 • Arzobispo Meriño 452 • 809 682 3309 • Open 9am–6pm Mon–Sat, 9am–1pm Sun • www.amberworldmuseum.com*

Amber

4 Agora Mall

This environmentally-friendly mall offers a wide range of shops, a Jumbo Supermarket, an indoor amusement park, and a cinema. There are 7 self-contained restaurants and over 20 restaurants in the food court. The mall is fully air-conditioned and has parking space for about 1,800 cars. ⊛ *Map J1 • Av Kennedy on corner of Av Abraham Lincoln*

5 Galeria de Ambar, Puerto Plata

Located underneath a small amber museum is this exquisite jewelry and gift store, where you can buy not only amber but also larimar, the beautiful turquoise stone found only in the southwest of the Dominican Republic. This hidden gem is the ideal place in which to buy something that is truly Dominican. ⊛ *Map C1 • Calle 12 de Julio • 809 586 2101 • Open 8:30am–6pm Mon–Fri, 9am–1pm Sat*

6 Flea Market, Santo Domingo

Sunday mornings see the hustle-bustle of several *mercados de pulgas* in the capital. The outdoor gatherings at the bottom of Avenida Luperón and Avenida 30 de Mayo offer unlikely household implements, occasional antiques, day-to-day clothing, and cheap food.
⊗ *Open 7am–noon Sun*

7 Calle del Sol, Santiago

The long, straight street of this commercial center cuts through downtown, lined with old-fashioned department stores, banks, and street stalls. You'll find almost everything including "designer" sunglasses from China *(see p15)*. ⊗ *Map C2*

8 Boutique del Fumador

Sample some of the finest cigars or watch them being rolled in the shop window and on the second floor. Monte Cristo, Cohiba, and Caoba cigars are sold here. ⊗ *Map N5 • Calle El Conde 109 • 809 685 6425 • Open 9am–7pm Mon–Sat, 10am–3:30pm Sun*

9 Beach Markets

Big tourist resorts such as Bávaro and Bayahibe often allow small traders to set up informal markets. These are places to find genuine bargains away from the overpriced malls. Look out for rum, music, cheap Haitian art and fabrics *(see p23)*.

10 Colmados

The friendly little corner stores doubling as bars are the place to go for day-to-day items such as drinks, snacks or soap. You might not find much to buy, but you'll find the rum cheaper than in tourist stores *(see p53)*.

Top 10 Buys

1 Amber
The golden resin makes beautiful jewelry, but before buying make sure that the piece is authentic.

2 Larimar
This cool blue mineral is mined exclusively here and is sold uncut or as jewelry.

3 Cigars
Some aficionados rate hand-rolled Dominican cigars even higher than Cuban and they are certainly better value.

4 Rum
White, golden, or *añejo* (dark and aged), each has its appeal and is good value.

5 Wood Carvings
Bowls and plates made from the hardwood *guayacán* tree are attractively solid and extremely colorful.

6 Taíno Artifacts
Not the original ones, of course, but well-crafted replicas can be found on sale in museums and gift shops.

7 Carnival Masks
The best known are the multicolored *papier-mâché* devil masks from La Vega and Santiago, also available in Santo Domingo.

8 Haitian Art
Though much of it is mass-produced kitsch, you are likely to fall for a resplendent country scene.

9 CDs
The choice of merengue and bachata albums is bewildering. Ask the shop assistant to play a few.

10 Coffee
Some of the best mountain-grown aromatic beans in the Caribbean are sold in vacuum-sealed tins at fairly reasonable prices.

Left & Right **La Atarazana, Santo Domingo**

Restaurants

Casa Veintiuno, Sosúa
This Belgian-owned stylish restaurant offers an extensive international menu. All of the dishes are made with fresh ingredients and the wine list has been well chosen. The open kitchen allows guests to watch the chefs at work and adds to the atmosphere. ✎ Map D1 • Calle Piano 1, • Tavares, Sosúa • 829 342 8089 or 809 341 8551 • Open 6–11pm Wed–Sun; lunch by reservation only • $$$$$

El Conuco, Santo Domingo
Dominican food is the specialty at this restaurant, which looks like a rustic dwelling. Opt for the fixed-price buffet, which is more extensive in the evening than at lunchtime, or eat à la carte. Dancers and musicians perform in native costume (see p76). ✎ Map M3 • Casimiro de Moya 152 • 809 686 0129 • Open 11:30am–midnight daily • $$$$$

La Atarazana, Santo Domingo
Housed in an old colonial building and known for both local and international dishes, especially seafood, this is a pleasant place to stop for lunch while sight-seeing, or for dinner. ✎ Map P5 • Calle La Atarazana • 809 689 2900 • Open 11am–midnight Mon–Sat • $$$

Mesón de la Cava, Santo Domingo
Dine in a great setting – a natural cave, with strategic lighting in tunnels, and antechambers. La Cava is popular for steaks and seafood (see p76). ✎ Map J4 • Av Mirador del Sur 1 • 809 533 2818 • Open 9am–11pm Tue–Sun • $$$$$

Rancho Camp David, Santiago
This high-class restaurant has a wonderful view of Santiago and the Cibao valley. Its delicious meat and fish dishes are very popular. There's also a small hotel here (see p85). ✎ Map C2 • Carretera Luperón 7.5 km • 809 276 6400 • Open from breakfast to dinner • $$$$

Mi Corazón, Las Terrenas
Considered one of the best restaurants in the country, Mi Corazón exudes a typical colonial ambience. The menu fuses European and Dominican flavors and focuses mostly on seafood. ✎ Map F2 • Calle Duarte 7 (Principal), Esquina Carretera Coson, Las Terrenas, Samaná • 809 240 5329 • Open 7:30pm–midnight Tue–Sun • $$$$$

Sophia
Located in the Piantini district, this upscale restaurant is one of the best that Santo Domingo has to offer. The menu features burgers, churrasco steaks, exquisite racks of lamb, and fresh seafood. ✎ Map J2 • Paseo de los Locutores, Piantini • 809 620 1001 • Open 11am–midnight Sun–Thu, 11am–3am Fri & Sat • $$$$$

Pez Dorado, Santiago
A well-established bistro, popular with the upper-income residents, particularly for family

Sunday lunches. The menu is a combination of Chinese, Dominican, and international dishes. The food and wines are excellent, and portions generous. ✆ Map C2 • Calle del Sol 43, Santiago de los Caballeros • 809 582 2518 • Open 9am–midnight daily • $$$$

9 Aroma de La Montaña, Jarabacoa

Situated in mountainous Jamaca de Dios, this restaurant has stunning views over the Cibao Valley from a 360-degree revolving platform. The menu features Dominican and international dishes made with organic produce grown in the owner's garden. ✆ Map C3 • Jamaca de Dios • 829 452 6879 • 11am–10pm Sun–Thu, 11am–11pm Fri & Sat • $$$$$

10 Pat'e Palo, Santo Domingo

Located in a historic building, Pat'e Palo is said to be the oldest tavern in the Americas. European-style fish and meat dishes are served on a terrace that offers wonderful views over the Zona Colonial. ✆ Map P5 • Calle La Atarazana 25, Plaza España • 809 687 8089 • Open noon–1am daily • $$$$$

Pretty interiors of the Pat'e Palo

Top 10 Restaurants by the Sea

1 Las Salinas
Has a varied menu from substantial burgers to lobster at US$30 (see p113).

2 Adrian Tropical, Santo Domingo
A place to try local specialties such as mofongo (see p76).

3 El Paraíso, Playa El Valle
Serves delicious fish and shrimp from a beach shack under palm trees (see p104).

4 Capitán Cook, Bávaro
Choose your own freshly caught lobster or fish at this lively restaurant (see p77).

5 Neptuno's Club, Boca Chica
Seafood restaurant built out over the water with a replica caravel for a bar (see p77).

6 On the Waterfront, Sosúa
Offers glorious views at sunset (see p58).

7 Atlantis, Las Terrenas
The former personal cook of French President François Mitterrand offers fine French cuisine on the beach of Playa Bonita (see p104).

8 Villa Serena, Las Galeras
A romantic restaurant with idyllic views (see p133).

9 Playa del Pescador, Guayacanes
Popular seafood restaurant located on the beach. ✆ Map F4 • 809 526 2613 • Open 8am–11pm daily • $$$

10 La Casa del Pescador
Serves fresh fish and seafood including an excellent paella for two. ✆ Map D1 • Cabarete • 809 571 0760 • Open 10am–11pm daily • $$$$

Left **Live music at Casa de Teatro** Right **On the Waterfront sign, Sosúa**

TOP 10 **Bars**

1 Atarazana 9, Santo Domingo
Time your sightseeing in the old city so that you can have an evening drink here. It's one of the many historic buildings around the Alcázar de Colón (see p9) that have been converted into a bar or restaurant. ◈ Map P4 • Zona Colonial • 809 689 2900 • Open 8pm–3am Tue–Thu, 8pm–4am Fri–Sun

2 El Rey del Falafel, Santo Domingo
More than an ordinary pub, this is a meeting point for artists and musicians, and on weekends there are sessions of live music too. Enjoy an ice-cold beer or tropical fruit cocktail with your falafel or hummus. ◈ Map N6 • Calle Padre Billini 352 & corner of Sanchez • 809 688 9714 • Open 11am–midnight daily

3 Bailey's Bar & Restaurant, Sosúa
A breakfast bar in the morning, Bailey's serves snacks at lunchtime. In the evening, it shifts into bar mode. ◈ Map D1 • Calle Dr Alejo Martínez, El Batey • 809 571 3085 • Open 8am until late daily

4 Roadway, Puerto Plata
During the day this is a restaurant, while at night it converts to a disco with three bars – two inside and one outside. A popular place for meeting the locals, especially on weekends. ◈ Map C1 • Playa Dorada Plaza • 809 320 4502 • Open 9am–4am

5 On the Waterfront, Sosúa
Primarily a restaurant, this bar on the cliff-top overlooking the sea is a great place for a sunset cocktail. There is live music on Saturdays. ◈ Map D1 • Calle Dr Rosen 1 • 809 571 3024 • Open noon–midnight daily • Happy hour 5–7pm

Beer

6 Mojitos, Las Terrenas
Renowned for its namesake cocktail, this famous bar on a sandy beach in the Samaná Peninsula is surrounded by palm trees, and serves Cuban and Dominican food (see p105). ◈ Map F2 • Punta Popi • Open 9am–10pm daily

7 José Oshay's Irish Beach Pub, Cabarete
Walk through José Oshay's shopping village, off the main road, to reach this beachfront bar. Food is available, but it's basically a drinking spot, packed at night with windsurfers burning candles at both ends after a busy day on the waves (see p91). ◈ Map D1 • Cabarete Beach • 809 571 0775 • Open 8am–1am daily

8 Casa de Teatro, Santo Domingo
Famous Dominican musicians such as Juan Luis Guerra started

their careers on the stage of this private bar and theater. You can hear live music in the courtyard on Thursday to Saturday nights. It also puts on art exhibitions and plays. ◈ *Map P6 • Calle Arzobispo Meriño 110 • 809 689 3430 • Open 7pm–midnight Sun–Thu, 7pm–3am Fri & Sat*

Rocky's Rock and Blues Bar
Sip on refreshing tropical cocktails, dine on American-style dishes, listen to great music, and mingle with an interesting crowd at this bar and restaurant. ◈ *Map D1 • Calle Dr Rosen 24, Sosúa • 809 571 2951 • Open 8am until late daily*

Hemingway's Café, Puerto Plata
The bar is decorated along the theme of Ernest Hemingway, with nautical and sportfishing paraphernalia around the walls. On weekends there's live music and some karaoke, otherwise a DJ plays rock, Latin electronic, and house music. It's popular with visitors and tourists from the resorts who want a change of scenery. ◈ *Map C1 • Playa Dorada Shopping Mall • 809 320 2230 • Open 10am–1am Mon–Thu, 10am–3am Fri–Sun*

Hemingway's Café, Playa Dorada

Top 10 Drinks

1 Presidente Beer
This deservedly world-famous lager-style brew is usually served so cold that it's almost frozen.

2 Rum
Dominican rum is among the Caribbean's best, and is the national drink *(see p55)*.

3 Ron Ponch
Rum disguised with sweet fruit juices and cordials, and therefore to be treated with extreme caution.

4 Coffee
Locally grown coffee is delicious drunk as a simple espresso, but hotels often offer instant grains.

5 Coconut Milk
Cool coconut milk drunk straight from a freshly chopped nut is the quintessential Caribbean thirst quencher.

6 Juices
An infinite variety of tropical fruits *(see p65)* are turned into irresistible juices, which are often very sweet.

7 Batidas
Fruit juice mixed in the blender with crushed ice and condensed milk to produce smoothies.

8 Morir Soñando
"To die dreaming" is the poetic name for a blend of orange juice, milk, and ice.

9 Refrescos
The general term for soda-style soft drinks of different colors and degrees of sweetness.

10 Ponche de Frutas
An alcohol-free punch of mixed juices makes a refreshing change from its rum-blended relative.

Left **Merengue venue, Santo Domingo** Right **Platinum, Santo Domingo**

🔟 Nightlife & Merengue Venues

1 El Rinconcito de Don Guillermo, Santo Domingo

Next to the ruins of the Monasterio de San Francisco is a small *colmado* where you can sit outside with a cold beer and listen to music on the juke box. There's a live merengue band on Sundays.
🕙 Map P5 • Calle Hostos & corner of Emiliano Tejera • 809 688 3110 • Open 8am–11pm daily, live music 5–10pm Sun

2 Imagine, Punta Cana

With live music and DJs, Imagine has established a reputation as the hotspot of the east coast. In high season, it hosts themed evenings. A shuttle service to and from the main hotels of the region is available.
🕙 Map H4 • Carretera Arena Gorda, Coco Loco Friusa, Punta Cana • 809 466 1185 • Open 11pm until late Tue–Sun

3 Jet Set, Santo Domingo

A casual place where Dominicans come for good Latin dance music. Look out for live merengue bands on Mondays

Jet Set, Santo Domingo

(see p75). 🕙 Map J4 • Independencia 2253 • 809 537 9337/9599 • Open 7pm–1am Sun–Thu, 6pm–3am Fri & Sat

4 Avenida Venezuela, Santo Domingo East

East of Santo Domingo's cosmopolitan center, across the Ozama river which dissects the city, is the place to go for authentic Dominican nightlife. Lively and distinct, this buzzing nightspot boasts vibrant music, spirited dancers, and a carnival atmosphere amid the collection of Latin dance clubs that line the street.
🕙 Map P1

5 Gran Almirante Hotel & Casino, Santiago

The Spanish restaurants and bars here offer meals or tapas, and there is a casino for adult amusement. The real action begins at around 11pm, however, when Dominicans – dressed smartly but provocatively – arrive for a good time.
🕙 Map C3 • Estrella Sadhalá, Santiago de los Caballeros 10 • 809 580 1992 • Open 11am until late daily

6 Rancho Tipico, Puerto Plata

This is a typically friendly Dominican dance place where you can meet the locals and practise your merengue, bachata, and salsa dance steps.
🕙 Map C1 • West, Autopista Puerto Plata–Santiago, after Zona Franca • Open 6pm until late daily

7 D'Classico, Sosúa

A large, fun disco where they play a mixture of merengue, bachata, Latin music, rock, and pop. At weekends it's mainly Dominican music, which attracts local youth keen to befriend foreigners and teach them how to dance (see p91).
Map D1 • Calle Pedro Clisante • Open 11pm–2am Sun–Thu, 10pm–3am Fri & Sat

Salsa

8 Coco Bongo, Playa Dorada

Live music starts at 10pm in this most popular of discos in the hotel complex of Playa Dorada. Various DJs play a mix of merengue, bachata, and salsa as well as rock and pop (see p91).
Map C1 • Plaza Playa Dorada • 809 320 2259 • Open 11pm until late daily

9 Hard Rock Café, Santo Domingo

A 'dog-tag' dress from Rihanna and mementos from Justin Timberlake, Jimmy Hendrix, and Elvis Presley line the walls of this 285-seat eatery, which boasts a rooftop terrace and VIP bar, and serves tasty American fast food (see p75).
Map J2 • Blue Mall, Av Winston Churchill, corner Av Gustavo Mejia Ricart • 809 606 7771 • Open noon–midnight Sun–Thu, noon–1am Fri & Sat

10 Platinum, Santo Domingo

A favorite with students from the nearby university, this night-club showcases a variety of live music acts, as well as DJs playing a mix of merengue, salsa, bachata, and reggaeton. Map K4 • 2nd Floor, Av Independencia, corner Av Alma Mater, Plaza Mirador II • 809 508 0115 • Open 7pm–4am Mon & Thu–Sat

Top 10 Merengue & Bachata Performers

1 **Hector Acosta "El Torito"** One of the most popular merengue and bachata artists in the world.

2 **Fulanito** This band mixes merengue with rap and hip-hop to produce "merenhouse" music.

3 **Juan Luis Guerra** An international superstar, the classically trained musician blends jazz-influenced merengue and sentimental bachata music.

4 **Milly Quezada** "The Queen of Merengue" has been an internationally popular singer and bandleader since the 1970s.

5 **Los Hermanos Rosario** A six-brother boy band from Higüey, which recorded several bestselling albums in its 1980s heyday.

6 **Toño Rosario** Formerly of the Hermanos Rosario, Toño, a.k.a. El Cuco, is a modern-day merengue superstar.

7 **Luis Segura** Dubbed "the Father of Bachata", the veteran Segura sings the tear-jerking Dominican version of C&W.

8 **Ruby Perez** Singer of romantic songs and known as "the highest voice in merengueros".

9 **Wilfrido Vargas** Multitalented composer and performer who has popularized merengue across Latin America.

10 **Johnny Ventura** An extrovert exponent of brass-dominated dance music.

Left **Bandera Dominicana** Right **Delicious fish stew**

Dishes of the Dominican Republic

Bandera Dominicana

The closest thing to a national dish, the so-called "Dominican Flag" doesn't exactly copy the colors of the nation's emblem. However, it does provide a nutritious mix of red beans; rice; beef, pork, or chicken; and salad. Occasionally, avocado or fried plantain are also added. This combination is available every-where, and is extremely filling.

Sancocho

A close relative of stews made in Colombia and Venezuela, real *sancocho* contains no fewer than five different sorts of meat (chicken, goat, pork, beef, and sausage) as well as a medley of vegetables and spices. It's a dish for very special occasions, also reflecting the country's mixed European and African heritage.

Crayfish

Chivo Asado

The humble goat, seen browsing at every roadside, is a firm favorite, especially when roasted into a state of extreme tenderness after being marinated in rum and spices. This delicacy is normally reserved for holidays and celebrations, when it might be eaten with traditional flat rounds of cassava bread.

Lambi

The country's seafood, including sea bass, lobster, and shrimp, is varied and delicious. Of almost legendary status among locals, however, is *lambi* or conch, served cold with a vinaigrette or hot in a tomato and garlic stew. This large mollusk may seem a little chewy, but its appeal lies in its supposedly aphrodisiac qualities.

Mangú

A wholesome and extremely satisfying breakfast staple, this has nothing to do with mangoes but is a very filling plate of mashed plantain, drizzled with olive oil and sometimes seasoned with fried onions or cheese. A welcome break from imitation American breakfasts, this will match the largest of morning appetites.

Mofongo

Another calorie-laden plantain favorite, this is eaten as a side dish for lunch or dinner. Plantains are fried, mashed, and mixed with garlic and pieces of fried pork *(chicharrones)*. The delicious end result can be filled with a sauce such as prawns or beef, but is also good on its own.

Mondongo

Not under any circumstances to be confused with *mofongo*, mondongo is a formidable dish of pig's tripe, stewed in a tomato and garlic sauce. It has its fans among

Dominicans, especially as a Sunday brunch treat, as it is supposed to help cure the most stubborn of hangovers.

8 Asopao

A Dominican cross between a thick soup, a gumbo, and a Spanish paella, this mix of rice, chicken stock and spices can be served with chicken or seafood. A slightly less liquid version is called *locrio*, again featuring rice, vegetables and your choice of meat or seafood.

9 Casabe

Passed down by the indigenous Tainos, the making of cassava flour involves an intricate process of removing toxic cyanide residues by grating and drying the starch-filled tubers. The flour is then used to make a bread with a hard biscuit-like texture that can be eaten as a side dish or snack.

10 Dulce de Leche

Of all the ultra-sweet desserts beloved by Dominicans, this is by far the most widespread, a simple but irresistible blend of whole milk and sugar stirred together over a low heat until it reaches a cream-like consistency. Look out for variations on this sweet-toothed theme involving coconut and candied fruits.

Asopao

Top 10 Snacks

1 Pastelitos
Small but tasty pasties or turnovers filled with a savory center of minced beef, chicken or cheese.

2 Empanadas
A similar deep-fried turnover filled with meat or cheese, but this can be made with yucca flour.

3 Quipes
Another standard street snack, featuring Middle East-inspired cracked wheat rissoles stuffed with meat.

4 Yaniqueques
A local distortion of Johnny Cakes, this version is a sort of fried round flour bread served hot.

5 Chicharones
Deep-fried pieces of crunchy pork rind or crackling; sometimes chicken pieces are also used.

6 Chimichurris
A more hearty snack of slices of pork cut from a joint and eaten in a sandwich.

7 Batatas
Baked sweet potatoes are cooked out of the skin. Can be eaten either hot or cold.

8 Fritos Maduros
A Dominican version of fries, these are chunks of deep-fried ripe plantain, sprinkled with a little salt.

9 Tostones
Fried plantains again, but of the unripe type and more savoury, fried once, flattened, and refried.

10 Coconut Water
Drunk through a hole in the soft green coconut and sold almost everywhere, this is an incredibly refreshing drink to beat the heat.

left **Trunk of the mahogany tree** Right **Bougainvillea**

Trees & Flowers

1 Mahogany
This valuable, hard, red-brown wood has been logged and exported ever since the Spanish first established a colony here. It is quite rare in most parts, but you can still see plenty of *caoba* trees, some up to 60 ft (18 m) high, in the Cordillera Central (see p80).

2 Hispaniolan Royal Palm
The elegant royal palm is found throughout the island. Measuring up to 60 ft (18 m), its graceful appearance is matched by its usefulness, as it provides a lot of wood for house building.

3 Calabash
A small evergreen tropical tree with a strange nocturnal reproductive system – the calabash's flowers bloom only at night, when they are pollinated by bats. The fruits that develop in clusters along the trunk and branches have a hard green wooden shell, which since Taino times has been used as a utensil and ornament.

4 Creolean Pine
The only pine widespread in the Caribbean, this tree flourishes at altitudes above 6,500 ft (1,981 m), as on the flanks of Pico Duarte. The dense forests of the interior are filled with the distinctive fresh odor of Creolean pine, creating an illusion of the Alps in the tropics.

Calabash tree

5 Sea Grape
Ubiquitous along the wilder beaches, this tough shrub looks twisted and stunted but thrives in the inhospitable terrain of sand and salt water. Some grow tall and provide a welcome shade. The so-called grapes, though edible, are extremely sour and taste better when made into a jelly.

6 Orchid
Orchids are big business around Jarabacoa and Constanza, where they are grown commercially for the North American market. The beautiful flowers also grow profusely in the wild, especially in the humid climate of the higher reaches of the Parque Nacional Sierra de Baoruco, where there are over 150 species.

7 Bromeliad
A large grouping of eye-catching plants, of which the pineapple is a member, and increasingly popular as exotic indoor ornamentals. Here, they grow wild, either in the ground or sprouting from a tree, shrub, or even from a telegraph post.

8 Bougainvillea

The bright red, purple, white, or pink flowers of this spectacular shrub are in fact large bracts that surround the small and inconspicuous flowers. A great favorite as a garden plant because it flowers for most of the year, it is actually a native of South America and was imported to the Caribbean.

9 Hortensia

Also a common female name in the Dominican Republic, the mop-headed hortensia is a very popular plant, having been imported from Japan. Such is the quantity of these flowers growing around the central town of Bonao that it is widely known as the Villa de las Hortensias.

10 Prickly Pear Cactus

One of the many types of spiny plants that cling precariously to life in the parched desert regions around Barahona and Monte Cristi is the *opuntia*, known among the locals as *tuna*. It produces pretty flowers on its plump water-retaining pads before the pinkish and very hard-to-handle fruits appear. Although the fruits are eaten in many countries, they are not a part of Dominican cuisine.

Hortensia or hydrangea

Top 10 Fruits

1 Guineo

The local name for bananas, but unlike the large starchy plantains the *guineos* are the smaller and sweeter variety.

2 Lechoza

The very popular and succulent papaya or papaw, normally served with banana at breakfast.

3 Guanábana

A variety of sugar apple or *sweetsop*, its sweet white flesh tastes rather like vanilla.

4 Jagua

This light brown fruit with a distinctive sweet taste is a member of the sugary custard-apple family.

5 Caimito

A star apple. The round, usually yellow fruit contains a sweet, sticky pulp.

6 Mamey

The brown-skinned mamey-apple has orange, red, or reddish-brown flesh that makes an amazingly appetizing *batida*.

7 Zapote

The flesh of the zapote tastes like a cross between a banana and a peach.

8 Piña

The familiar pineapple is locally grown and is a firm favorite not only in milkshakes but also at buffets.

9 Chinola

This is a Dominican term for the passion fruit. Though rich in vitamins, it requires a spoonful of sugar to balance its sharpness.

10 Tamarindo

The tamarind's mushy flesh tastes sour when raw, but is often cooked and used to make delicious drinks.

American crocodile at Lago Enriquillo

🔟 Animal Life

1 American Crocodile

Up to 15 ft (4.5 m) in length, these crocs can look fearsome, but are in fact much more timid than their African or Australian relatives. They live up to 50 years on a diet of fish, waterfowl, and small mammals, thriving in the protected salt-water environment of Lago Enriquillo.

2 Rhinoceros Iguana

This big lizard, which grows up to 4-ft (1.2-m) long, gets its name from a horn-like bump on its nose. Naturally shy, they have become used to humans on the Isla Cabritos (see p26), but normally seek refuge from the heat in burrows. They bask in the sun to become active and live on very sparse vegetation.

3 Leatherback Turtle

An endangered species, the leatherback has no shell, but rather a series of bony plates covered with a leathery skin. These creatures can be over 6 ft (1.8 m) and weigh some

Iguana

800 lb (363 kg). They lay hundreds of eggs on remote beaches but are illegally hunted for meat and eggs.

4 Solenodon

You are unlikely to see one of these long-nosed ant-eating mammals in the wild, as they are rare, extremely shy, and nocturnal. They are also now a threatened species, largely because their habitat is shrinking, and they are easy prey for dogs and other predators. A few can still be seen in captivity.

5 Hutia

Another shy mammal, the endemic *hutia* looks rather like a rat, but it's actually a rabbit-sized herbivore that seeks refuge either in caves or in trees. Increasingly endangered by deforestation, it lives in the more remote and forested districts of the Parque Nacional del Este (see p41) and the Parque Nacional Los Haitises (see p33).

6 Lizard

Reptiles of all shapes and sizes have adapted to the island's varied ecosystems. The diverse variety of the species ranges from the hefty 4-ft (1.2-m) iguanas and chunky geckos to the tiny 1.6-cm jaragua gecko, which was discovered in 1998 on the isolated Isla Beata of the southwest coast. Don't be surprised to have a lizard or two visit your room.

7 Tree Frog

Popular among the locals as a *coqui*, the tiny greenish-brown frog is one of several similar species known for their surprisingly loud choruses during the hours of darkness. One of the most evocative of Caribbean sounds, the tireless nocturnal singing of tree frogs becomes louder after a heavy downpour.

Tree frog

8 Whale

Samaná Bay and the Banco de la Plata (Silver Bank), areas some 60-miles (97-km) northeast of Puerto Plata, are the preferred mating and calving grounds of humpback whales, which can grow up to a staggering 50 ft (15 m) and weigh 40 tons. It is a delight to see them leap out of the water.

9 Manatee

The rare and protected sea cow is the gentle giant of the ocean. Shy and vegetarian, it can reach 12 ft (3.6 m) in length, and rises to the sea's surface every five minutes to breathe air. It's hard to believe that this bulbous and whiskery creature was once mistaken for a mermaid.

10 Butterflies

Almost 300 species of butterfly have been identified, but it is thought there are many more, especially in the remote mountain terrain of the Sierra de Baoruco. The arid southwest is home to hundreds of colorful species, including some rare swallowtails and monarchs, attracting growing numbers of lepidopterists.

Top 10 Birds

1 Hispaniolan Woodpecker
Known as the *carpintero*, this handsome yellow and brown bird is unique to the island.

2 Hispaniolan Parakeet
Though an endangered species, it is instantly recognizable from its bright green feathers with red patches.

3 Hispaniolan Emerald Hummingbird
Found in the mountainous interior, the female species is lighter in hue than the black-breasted male.

4 Hispaniolan Trogon
A multicolored little bird, with a gray breast, red belly, green back, and a black-and-white tail.

5 Cattle Egret
The heron-like white bird can be seen in almost every field, and especially around flea-ridden cattle.

6 Turkey Vulture
No great beauty with its bare red face, it is nevertheless a useful carrion eater.

7 Flamingo
Pink and elegant in flight, this is the most attractive of the country's many estuary and lagoon birds.

8 Palm Chat
The brown *sigua palmera* is the national bird, nesting high up in the foliage of a palm tree.

9 Red-tailed Hawk
The versatile and efficient raptor that feeds on small mammals and reptiles is actually a buzzard.

10 Frigate Bird
This magnificent coal-black sea bird has a red throat that expands dramatically during its mating rituals.

Following pages **Rowboats and yachts in a lagoon, Bayahibe**

AROUND THE DOMINICAN REPUBLIC

DOMINICAN REPUBLIC'S TOP 10

Left **The Malecón, Santo Domingo** Center **Los Tres Ojos** Right **Boca Chica Beach**

Santo Domingo & the South Coast

FROM THE BUSTLING CAPITAL CITY *to the huge expanses of beach that make up the Costa del Coco, the Dominican Republic's South Coast is an intriguing mix of tourist activity and natural beauty. The southeast contains the country's traditional sugar territory, with huge plantations stretching to the horizon. This is also the heartland of baseball culture, centered around La Romana and San Pedro de Macorís, where local kids dream of making it big in the United States. Some of the country's most established seaside resorts are here, as well as the modern complexes*

of Bávaro and Punta Cana, offering a choice of quiet swimming or crowded people-watching. Most of the coastline can be reached by the scenic Carretera 3, known as the Las Americas highway, which runs adjacent to the sea, but the remote wilderness of the Parque Nacional del Este is only accessible by boat.

Statue of Fray Montesino, Santo Domingo

🔟 Sights

1	Santo Domingo	6	San Pedro de Macorís
2	Los Tres Ojos	7	La Romana
3	Acuario Nacional	8	Bayahibe
4	Boca Chica	9	Parque Nacional del Este
5	Juan Dolio	10	Punta Cana/Bávaro

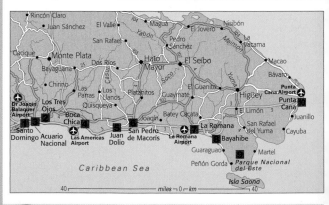

Santo Domingo

1 La Capital has something for everyone, from colonial-era streets steeped in history to state-of-the-art shopping malls. A patchwork of ancient and modern, the sprawling city lives life at a frantic pace, with gridlocked streets and other urban challenges. But there are quiet corners and shady plazas in the Zona Colonial; extensive parks offering fresh air, peace, and quiet; and the magnificent seaside Malecón, the favorite playground of Santo Domingo's inhabitants (see pp8–11).

Los Tres Ojos

2 The Three Eyes are a complex of *cenotes*, or karst caves containing subterranean mini-lagoons, stalactites, and stalagmites. What appears to be three lakes is, in fact, a single one, taking different colors under different lights in four caverns. Steps lead steeply down to the first cave, from where walkways and a pulley-powered vessel take visitors through the under-ground system. Reputedly a

Boaters at Boca Chica Beach

Taino holy site, the place is surprisingly unspoilt despite large numbers of tourists, and the last of the "eyes" offers a spectacular natural landscape of tropical vegetation, sheer rock faces, and green-tinged water. ◎ Map E4 • Av Las Américas/Parque Mirador del Este • Open 9am–5pm daily • Adm

Acuario Nacional

3 This technically impressive installation uses natural seawater to fill its various tanks, displaying an enormous and colorful range of tropical marine life. You can also walk through a viewing tunnel to get close to the sharks, barracudas, stingrays, and other underwater creatures. A pleasant snack bar looks over the sea (see p36).

Boca Chica

4 The easiest beach to reach from Santo Domingo is a boisterous and unpretentious place, verging on the raucous at weekends when tens of thousands of people escape from the capital to swim and listen to music. During the week it's a lot quieter, but even then there's no shortage of bars and restaurants. There are a number of hotels and guesthouses, too, offering good-value accommodation. The main draw is the beach (see p37), a lovely strip of sand set in a protective bay with clear water.

Stalactite formation in Los Tres Ojos caves

Left **Playa Juan Dolio** Right **Victorian houses along the Malecón, San Pedro de Macorís**

Juan Dolio
What was once a long strip of hotels along the beachfront has been replaced by a stretch of stunning high-rise apartment blocks. Most of these modern flats are owned by Dominicans from the capital, who descend on the town on weekends. It is relatively quiet during the week. Much of the action revolves around the beaches, which range from the fairly rocky to the sublimely sandy. ◈ *Map F4*

San Pedro de Macorís
A city whose fortunes have ebbed and flowed with world sugar prices, San Pedro was once the richest place in the country. Some of its Victorian buildings, such as the fire station and the mansions near the Parque Duarte, recall the boom years. But those times have gone – just a memory since San Pedro was battered by Hurricane Georges in 1998. Nowadays, the city produces world-class baseball players, some descended from the English-speaking migrants called *cocolos*, who settled on the island at the turn of the 19th century. ◈ *Map F4*

La Romana
This town boasts some pretty houses from the turn of the 19th century in the gridiron area around the Parque Central, as well as a large, sprawling market area where you will see all manner of everyday and exotic produce. The town is famed for its baseball players, but its real attractions for visitors are the nearby luxury resort of Casa de Campo and the unique replica Tuscan hilltop village of Altos de Chavón *(see pp24–5)*. ◈ *Map G4*

Bayahibe
Until the 1990s this was a quiet fishing village, with nothing much more than a few boats pulled up on the beach. But a wave of tourism has changed its character, bringing more amenities and many more visitors. Even so, the pastel-colored wooden huts and

Cocolo Heritage
The descendants of *cocolos*, who came to San Pedro from British Caribbean territories such as Tortola and Anguilla, still celebrate their heritage at the annual Fiesta of San Pedro, in June, with dancing and fancy costumes. The festivities are thought to derive from traditional English Christmas mummers' rituals involving miming and disguises.

gracious palm trees that line the beach still form a pretty scene. This is the best spot for scuba diving in the country and is the starting point for boat trips to the off-shore Isla Saona and Isla Catalina. Baya-hibe is also well endowed with eating and drinking spots. ◈ Map G4

9 Parque Nacional del Este
Adjacent to the well-trodden tourist track of Bayahibe and Playa Dominicus, this large expanse of protected natural wilderness covers over 100,000 acres (40,468 ha) of dry and mangrove forests and palm-lined beaches. The terrain on the mainland peninsula is much tougher going and less popular with tourists, but offers the determined explorer a wealth of birdlife and tropical vegetation as well as glimpses of Taino art and culture (see p41). ◈ Map G5

10 Punta Cana/Bávaro
The southeast tip of the country is everyone's idea of a desert island idyll – a panorama of soft sand and gently swaying palm trees facing a turquoise sea. Mass tourism has brought thousands of visitors each year to the complexes of Punta Cana and Bávaro, and the region has also developed into a thriving community of expats and Dominicans (see pp22–3). ◈ Map H4

Bayahibe

South Coast Drive

Morning

🕐 Leave congested Santo Domingo in a rental car after spending an hour admiring the sharks and manatee at the seaside **Acuario Nacional**. You could have a late breakfast or snack in the aquarium's cafeteria. A half-hour or so driving along the well-maintained Las Americas Highway 3, which passes the airport, brings you to the resort of **Boca Chica**. Take a look at its famous beach a few blocks to your right, traffic allowing, and have lunch at one of the beach-side shacks selling fish, conch, or shrimps.

Afternoon

Passing eastwards through tourist developments such as Juan Dolio and flat stretches of agricultural land, you reach **San Pedro de Macorís**, where you might take a look at some of the Victorian-era buildings. Or press on to **La Romana** for a quick tour of the old quarter around the **Parque Central** (see p24).

If returning to Santo Domingo, there's enough time to drive up to **Altos de Chavón** (see p25), the replica Tuscan village with designer boutiques and fantastic views over the river valley. Head back towards the capital, allowing a couple of hours before night falls.

Alternatively, drive back to the coastal road and turn right towards Bayahibe, where you can spend the night in one of the inexpensive hotels (advance booking recommended) or the beach-side complexes along Playa Viva Dominicus.

Left & Center **Isla Saona, Parque Nacional del Este**

TOP 10 Best of the Rest

1 Parque Mirador del Este
On the east bank of the Ozama, overlooked by the imposing Faro a Colón, this stretch of open parkland has a fine selection of trees and makes for a pleasant walk. ◈ Map E4

2 La Caleta Submarine Park
The main attraction for scuba divers and snorkelers is the *Hickory* wreck, deliberately sunk here, as well as coral reefs which are accessible from the Park's beach. ◈ Map E4 • Golden Arrow Diving Center: 809 566 7780

3 Playa Guayacanes
A quieter alternative to Boca Chica *(see p71)*, the long strip of soft sand and calm water, still home to a fishing community, attracts a mix of tourists and locals. ◈ Map F4

4 Tetelo Vargas Baseball Stadium
This concrete temple to the great Dominican passion is usually open during the day. ◈ Map F4 • Av Circunvalacion, San Pedro ◈ 809 529 3618

5 Playa Boca del Soco
The best beach in the San Pedro de Macorís area *(see p72)*, it marks the point where the Río Soco meets the sea. It also offers swimming in both salt and fresh water. ◈ Map F4

Playa Guayacanes

6 Isla Catalina
White sand beaches and coral beds beckon at Isla Catalina, where you can practise your snorkeling among the colorful exotic fish. ◈ Map G4 • Tropical Tours: 809 523 2029

7 Isla Saona
The most popular part of Parque Nacional del Este *(see p73)* can be easily reached by regular boat services. Despite the crowds, the island looks like a Robinson Crusoe fantasy. ◈ Map G5 • Association of Boat Owners: 809 710 7336

8 Casa de Ponce de León
This squat, stone house, built in 1505, belonged to Ponce de León, founder of Puerto Rico and Florida. ◈ Map H4 • San Rafael del Yuma • Open 9am–5pm Mon–Sat • Adm

9 Higüey
The sprawling modern city is nothing special, but the basilica *(see p49)*, built to replace the much older Iglesia San Dionisio, is certainly impressive. ◈ Map G4

10 La Otra Banda
This sleepy one-street village is popular with Punta Cana/Bávaro *(see pp22–3)* excursionists, largely because of its bright and photogenic wooden houses, built by immigrants from the Canary Islands. ◈ Map G4

Around the Dominican Republic – Santo Domingo & the South Coast

For further information on tour operators, log onto http://tropicaltoursromana.com.do

Left **Jet Set** Right **Sign for Parada 77**

🔟 Nightlife

Parada 77
A popular place in the Zona Colonial where crowds gather in the street and locals come to dance merengue and bachata. ◈ *Map P5 • Calle Isabela La Católica 255, Zona Colonial, Santo Domingo • 809 221 7880 • Open 8pm–midnight Sun–Thu, 7pm–2am Fri & Sat*

Hard Rock Café Punta Cana
Young people come here to soak up the lively rock atmosphere. ◈ *Map H4 • Plaza Palma Real, Carretera El Cortecito 57, Punta Cana • 809 552 0594 • Open 11:30am–2am daily*

Jet Set
A great place in Santo Domingo for both recorded and live Latin music – mostly traditional. Juan Luís Guerra songs are always played *(see p60)*.

Avenida Venezuela
The place to go for authentic Dominican music. Enjoy the amazing atmosphere of one of the upscale clubs or dance footloose in the street *(see p60)*.

Hard Rock Café Santo Domingo
You can listen to modern rock and pop music here or relax in front of the big TV screens that show popular musical performances and live sporting events *(see p61)*.

Montecristo Café
Named after the Count of Monte Cristo, this English-style pub and café offers hot and cold snacks. ◈ *Map J2 • Calle José Amado Soler esquina Abraham Lincoln, Santo Domingo • 809 542 5000 • Open 6pm–1am Mon–Thu, 6pm–4am Fri–Sun*

Secreto Musical Bar
Merengue, salsa, and bachata ballads are played, but, most notably, this is the headquarters of the Club Nacional de los Soneros, so there's lots of Cuban music, particularly son. ◈ *Map N2 • Baltazar de los Reyes esquina Pimentel, Santo Domingo • Open evenings until late*

Barceló Bávaro Casino
Five Barceló hotels share the facilities of a 24-hour casino, a theater featuring Las Vegas-style Tropicalísimo casino shows, and a disco which plays a variety of music. ◈ *Map H4 • Bávaro, Higüey • Disco: until 4am daily*

Hotel Be Live Hamaca
At this venue, the music's mostly Latin. American and English numbers are played occasionally. A well-equipped casino with tables and slot machines awaits those who enjoy gambling. ◈ *Map F4 • Calle Duarte 2 & corner of Carol, Boca Chica • Open 6am–4am daily*

Atarazana 9
Located by Alcázar de Colón *(see p9)*, Atarazana 9 is a café and bar offering live music and a relaxed atmosphere *(see p58)*. ◈ *Map P5*

Left & Center **Mesón de la Cava** Right **Adrian Tropical**

🔟 Restaurants, Santo Domingo

1 D'Luis Parrillada
You can get typical Dominican food in this charming open-air restaurant right by the sea. It's also famous for its grilled meats. 🔊 Map N6 • Av George Washington 25, Malecón • 809 686 2940 • Open 9am–midnight daily • $$

2 Mesón de Barí
Mesón offers excellent Dominican cuisine with a selection of typical local dishes. 🔊 Map P5 • Hostos 302 • 809 687 4091 • Open noon–midnight • $$$$$

3 Punto Italia
You can buy original foodstuffs from Italy as well as ordering prepared Italian food. Prices are reasonable. 🔊 Map K4 • Av Abraham Lincoln & corner of José Contreras • 809 532 6155 • Open 11am–11pm daily • $$$

4 Mesón de la Cava
Relish the experience of dining on delicious seafood inside a spectacular natural cave (see p56).

5 Lulú Tasting Bar
Enjoy a classic cocktail and share an amazing array of sliders, satay, shrips and other appetizers. 🔊 Map N6 • Calle Padre Billini 151 • 809 687 8360 • Open 6pm–3am daily • $$$$

6 La Briciola
A lovely colonial courtyard and terrace provides the perfect setting for dinner by candlelight. Italian cuisine is the specialty.

🔊 Map P6 • Arzobispo Meriño 152 • 809 688 5055 • Open noon–3pm, 6–11pm daily • $$$$$

7 Museo de Jamón
Not a museum as the name suggests, but a Spanish restaurant serving delicious tapas. 🔊 Map P5 • La Atarazana 17 • 809 688 9644 • Open noon–11pm • $$$$

8 Adrian Tropical
Local dishes such as *mofongo*, and international cuisine, in an attractive setting by the sea. 🔊 Map M4 • Av George Washington 5 • 809 221 1764 • Open 24 hours daily • $$$

9 El Conuco
Popular with tour groups and locals, El Conuco offers a good value buffet lunch and dinner. Traditional dance performances during busy periods (see p56). 🔊 Map M3 • Casimiro de Moya 152, Gazcue • 809 686 0129 • Open 11:30am–midnight • $$$

10 Conde de Peñalba
A great place for the special local dish, *la bandera Dominicana*. 🔊 Map P6 • Calle El Conde and corner of Arzobispo Meriño • 809 688 7121 • Open 7:15am–11pm daily • $$

La Casita, La Romana

🔟 Restaurants, South Coast

1 Neptuno's Club
Set right by the sea, with its dining area built out over the water. The bar is a replica caravel. Excellent fresh fish and seafood *(see p57)*. 🚫 *Map F4 • Calle Duarte 12, Boca Chica • 809 523 4703 • Open 11am–11pm • $$$$$*

2 Capitán Cook
A restaurant set on the sand in a shady spot under trees. Very popular for lobster (sold by weight), fish, paella and a jug of sangría, for a Spanish touch *(see p57)*. 🚫 *Map H4 • Playa El Cortecito, Bávaro • 809 552 0645 • Open 11am–11pm Tue–Sun • $$$$$*

3 La Loma
Clinging to the hillside, with panoramic views, this hotel is difficult to get to, but good for both snacks and meals. 🚫 *Map G3 • Calle La Loma, Miches • 809 553 5562 • Open for breakfast, lunch, & dinner • $$*

4 Jellyfish
Located on a stunning beach, this place serves an international menu, and specializes in seafood. 🚫 *Map H4 • between Melia (Caribe, Tropical) and IFA Resorts, Punta Cana • 809 840 7684 • Open 11am–11pm daily • $$$$*

5 Mare Nostrum
This inviting Italian restaurant has an open-air terrace overlooking the bay. On the menu is a varied selection of seafood dishes. 🚫 *Map G4 • Calle Juan Brito/Calle Principal, Bayahibe • 809 833 0055 • Open noon–4pm, 7–10:30pm daily • $$$$*

6 Deli Swiss
This tiny hideaway is famous for its gourmet offerings and superior wine selection. Owner and chef Walter Kleinert serves up delicious fresh meat and fish dishes. 🚫 *Map F4 • Playa Guayacanes, Calle Central 338, Juan Dolio • 809 526 1226 • Open 11am–8pm daily • $$$$*

7 La Casita Restaurant
Dine on fine Spanish cuisine including sumptuous seafood specialties, while enjoying breathtaking views over the marina. 🚫 *Map G4 • Marina Casa de Campo, La Romana • 809 523 3333 • Open 6–11pm, reservations required • $$$$$*

8 La Casita
The proprietors serve Italian and international cuisine, and specialize in seafood. The walls are adorned with a pretty collection of plates. 🚫 *Map G4 • Francisco R Doucu Dray 57, La Romana • 809 556 5932 • Open 11am–11:30pm Wed–Mon • $$*

9 Cappucino Mare
A five-star eatery with service to match. Enjoy the Italian-inspired menu, which specializes in fresh seafood. 🚫 *Map H4 • The Marina, Cap Cana • 809 468 4646 • Open noon–3pm, 7pm–midnight Wed–Mon • $$$$$*

10 La Yola
An excellent seafood and Mediterranean/Caribbean restaurant, beautifully situated over the water. 🚫 *Map H4 • Punta Cana Beach Resort • 809 959 2262 • Open noon–3pm, 7–10:30pm Wed–Mon • $$$$$*

Around the Dominican Republic – Santo Domingo & the South Coast

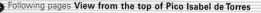

Following pages **View from the top of Pico Isabel de Torres**

Left **La Vega** Right **Mercado Modelo, Santiago**

The Central Highlands

ENTIRELY DIFFERENT IN TEMPERATURE *and atmosphere from the low-level capital and seaside resorts, the country's interior is dominated by the rugged mountain range known as the Cordillera Central, which arcs down from the Haitian border towards San Cristóbal. The highest point of the range is the Pico Duarte at 10,164 ft (3,098 m), but there are many other peaks and adjacent valleys, especially in and around the popular tourist bases of Jarabacoa and Constanza. Here, you can even feel the chill of an early morning frost, while a profusion of flowers and vegetables thrive in the temperate climate. Santiago is situated within easy reach of the mountains, separating them from the fertile farmland of the Cibao Valley, and from here it is a fascinating excursion westwards through the Highlands to the hilltop town of San José de las Matas.*

Exhibit, Museo de Arte, Bonao

🔟 Sights

1	Bonao	6	La Ciénega
2	La Vega	7	San José de las Matas
3	Santo Cerro	8	San Juan de la Maguana
4	Santiago	9	Coral de los Indios
5	The Dominican Alps	10	Las Matas de Farfán

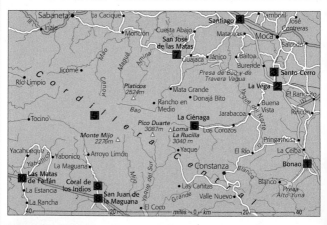

Discover more at www.dk.com

1 Bonao

A place historically dominated by mining, Bonao is not the prettiest site in the country, though it is strategically situated on the Autopista Duarte that connects Santo Domingo to Santiago. The Falconbridge plant, when operating, can be visited free of charge, but also explore the pretty mountain scenery around the town by taking the small road towards the Presa Alto Yuna, the nearby dammed lake. There are fine views of the Cordillera Central. ◈ *Map D3*

2 La Vega

One of the earliest European settlements, La Vega was an important base for gold-mining in the Cibao Valley during Columbus's time. After being flattened by an earthquake, it was rebuilt farther south. Little remains of its Victorian-era boom time, when some imposing public buildings appeared. The most conspicuous structure these days is the concrete modernist Catedral de la Concepción de La Vega, apparently intended to capture the spirit of the colonial period. La Vega really comes into its own each February, when it stages one of the country's most famous Carnival celebrations *(see p50)*, and the construction of masks from papier-mâché becomes an art form. ◈ *Map D2*

Santiago's cathedral

3 Santo Cerro

Commanding a spectacular view of the valley that Columbus dubbed La Vega Real (Royal Valley), the 19th-century church of Santo Cerro reputedly marks the spot where the Virgin made a miraculous intervention in 1495. The cross that she defended from burning by the Tainos was, according to legend, erected on the hillside by Columbus himself, and the church claims to preserve a fragment of the original crucifix. It's surrounded by ornate Catholic iconography *(see p46)*.

4 Santiago

Smaller and slower paced than the capital, Santiago is nonetheless a major metropolis of over one million people, with contrasting elements of wealth and poverty, old and new. The plush modern suburbs to the north are pleasant, but the city's real atmosphere and interest are concentrated in a relatively small downtown district around the Parque Duarte and the huge Monumento a los Héroes de la Restauracíon, joined by the main shopping street. It's also worth looking into Santiago's proud past as a major producer of sugar and tobacco, especially with a visit to a reconstructed cigar factory *(see pp14–15)*.

La Vega

5 The Dominican Alps

This is an ideal place for outdoor activities, ranging from hiking and horseback riding to challenging river-based sports, and the resorts of Jarabacoa and Constanza specialize in excursions. The climate and lack of urban spread also contribute to a wide and varied range of fauna and flora, making it a paradise for bird-watchers and botanists *(see pp12–13)*.

(see pp12–13)

View of Pico Duarte from La Ciénega

6 La Ciénega

The tiny rural village of La Ciénega de Manaboa is the starting point for the popular hike to the summit of Pico Duarte. The office for Parque Nacional Armando Bermúdez *(see p13)* is situated to the north of the village, and it is obligatory to register here and hire a guide. There is a rudimentary camping ground by the park office, where some climbers spend the night before setting off early the next morning. The Ciénega Trail is about 28 miles (45 kms) and usually takes around three days. Map C3

7 San José de las Matas

Another starting point for a Pico Duarte ascent, this airy and laid-back

Ripped Parrot

The strangely named *perico ripiao* (ripped parrot) is a style of merengue music developed in Santiago in the early 20th century. With lewd lyrics and an irresistible rhythm, it was frowned upon by polite society. Not surprisingly perhaps, as the Ripped Parrot was the name of a particularly notorious brothel.

mountain town provides a fascinating insight into everyday agricultural life. The surrounding countryside is dotted with coffee plantations and small farms, and the town itself acts as a trading center for local farmers. Apart from the *fiesta patronal*, staged every August, you can go on plenty of pleasant excursions to nearby rivers and swimming spots. The town also offers spectacular views over densely wooded hillsides and valleys, dotted with palm trees. Map C2

8 San Juan de la Maguana

A surprisingly large town lying in a fertile valley to the south of the Cordillera Central, San Juan is a busy agricultural center, surrounded by banana plantations and coffee farms. Its proximity to the Haitian border has brought problems over the centuries as invading armies occupied and destroyed the town. Today's architecture is modern, but there are also some turn-of-the-19th-century buildings around the Parque Central *(see p52)*, where a permanent buzz of outdoor buying and selling makes for an interesting walk. Map B3

Statue of San Juan de la Maguana

Las Matas de Farfán

Coral de los Indios

Reputed to be the site of an ancient Taino city, a large open space contains a ring of boulders with what seems to be a ceremonial slab in the middle. It was here that Anacaona, the legendary widow of Caonabo – who was tricked into captivity by the Spanish – attempted to galvanize anti-Spanish feeling among the differing Taino chieftains into a revolt. She was captured and executed, and the settlement destroyed. From what remains it is not clear how much is reconstructed, but the carved stone face on the slab looks authentic enough. ✎ *Map B3*

Las Matas de Farfán

The archetypal Dominican market town, Las Matas (literally roots) is supposed to be named after the tree under which the 18th-century merchant Farfán used to enjoy a siesta. It's still a sleepy sort of place, except on Saturdays, when the market brings crowds of *campesinos* into town for some bartering and gossip. There are few tourist sights as such, but Las Matas, as well as the surrounding countryside, gives a taste of small-town rural life. ✎ *Map B3*

A Morning in Santiago

After breakfast, head for the **Parque Duarte** *(see p14)*, the main downtown hub of activity. It's worth taking a look at some of the grand buildings lining the square, notably the Moorish-style **Centro de Recreo** and the **Palacio Consistorial** *(see p14)*, a Victorian-style building housing exhibitions. You can also hire a horse-drawn carriage, which should cost no more than US$12 for half an hour. Always negotiate a price before setting off.

The carriages normally run down the busy shopping street of **Calle del Sol** *(see p55)*, but you may prefer to walk the mile or so down this buzzing commercial thoroughfare. On the intersection of Calle del Sol and Avenida España you'll come across the **Mercado Modelo**, a cornucopia of tourist souvenirs.

As you reach the end of Calle del Sol and approach the **Monumento a los Héroes de la Restauración** *(see p15)*, look out for a couple of bars, such as **Puerto del Sol**, where you can stop for a drink.

Next, visit the massive monument to the dictator Trujillo (later re-branded as a memorial to independence fighters). The view from the top is worth the climb to the observation platform. End the day with a short visit to the **Centro León** (Av 27 de Febrero 146), a museum exhibiting photographs and paintings of important families from Santiago, as well as a replica of the La Aurora tobacco factory *(see p15)*.

Mangrove swamps, Parque Nacional del Este

Outdoor Activities

1 Hiking
The Dominican Alps *(see pp12–13 & 82)* are the perfect place for walking, whether short strolls or hikes. Most hotels can recommend a specialist operator for the more ambitious hikers who want something fairly challenging.

2 Horseback Riding
The region is well equipped for riding enthusiasts, with several outfits such as Rancho Baiguate offering top-class facilities. ⊗ *Rancho Baiguate: Map C3 • 809 574 6890 • www.ranchobaiguate.com*

White-water rafting near Jarabacoa

3 Cycling
Whether on or off road, cyclists will enjoy fantastic views as well as a warm welcome in villages, where you can always buy drinks.

4 Bird-Watching
The Cordillera Central is home to a number of exotic species, especially in the national parks. Look out for parrots and parakeets, as well as the Hispaniolan woodpecker and the emerald hummingbird.

5 White-Water Rafting
The fast-flowing Río Yaque del Norte near Jarabacoa *(see p12)* is a favorite place for this adrenaline-fueled sport, involving a fast descent through rocky canyons on a rubber raft shared by several paddlers.

6 Kayaking
The Río Yaque del Norte and the Jimenoa *(see p13)* are good kayaking rivers, with a mix of white water, sharp turns, and precipitous drops.

7 Canyoning
Jimenoa is the place for this energetic though rather challenging sport, which involves holding onto a rope and descending through canyons down a sheer rock face into the water below.

8 Cascading
In this exciting variant on canyoning, the participant jumps through a waterfall into the crystalline waters of the pool at the bottom.

9 Tubing
The low-budget version of rafting uses a large rubber ring. Swimmers are swept down the river, protected to some degree by the inflated tube.

10 Swimming
This can be enjoyed on the quieter stretches of the Cordillera Central's rivers as well as in many *balnearios* or swimming holes *(see p42)*.

All outdoor activities can be organized by Rancho Baiguate; call 809 574 6890, or log on to www.ranchobaiguate.com

Price Categories

Price categories include a three-course meal for one, a beer, and all unavoidable extra charges including tax.	$ under US$10
	$$ US$10–US$20
	$$$ US$20–US$30
	$$$$ US$30–US$40
	$$$$$ over US$40

Guinea fowl, a dish served in in Exquisiteses Dilenia

Places to Eat & Drink

Jarabacoa River Club
This club is popular with Dominicans at weekends for its buffet lunch on Sunday, as well as its pool. ◈ *Map C3 • Carretera Manaboa Pinal Quemodo, 3 miles (5 km) from Jarabacoa • 809 574 2456 • Open 10am–10pm Tue–Sun • $$$*

Restaurant Buen Sabor
A typical Dominican restaurant which attracts many local people who come for the good value dish of the day. ◈ *Map C3 • Entrada Av La Confluenca, Jarabacoa • 809 574 7071 • Open 8am–8pm daily • $$*

Picanha Rodizio Grill
If you like meat, this is the place to go. As much as you can eat of different cuts of high-quality meat for a fixed price. ◈ *Map C2 • Calle del Sol 13, Santiago • 809 971 5900 • Open 6pm–midnight Mon–Fri, noon–midnight Sat & Sun • $$$$*

La Tinaja
This popular meeting place for both foreigners and locals boasts a varied food menu and excellent coffee and fresh juices. ◈ *Map C3 • Ave Independencia, Jarabacoa • 809 574 2311 • Open 8am–11pm daily • $*

Comedor Luisa
Go for the *menú del día*, served with meat, rice, beans, and salad in this simple but tasty restaurant. ◈ *Map C3 • Calle Antonia María García 40, Constanza • 809 539 2174 • Open 8am–10pm daily • $$*

Exquisiteses Dilenia
Local meats such as lamb, rabbit, and guinea fowl are cooked here in various ways. ◈ *Map C3 • Calle Gaston F. Deligne 7, Constanza • 809 539 2213 • Open noon–10pm Tue–Sun • $$*

Rancho la Guazara
A Parque Recreacional popular day and night hangout with people bathing in the river and patronizing the bar, restaurant, and disco. ◈ *Map C3 • Vista del Yaque, 8 km from Jarabacoa on road to La Ciénaga, Manaboa • 829 630 4386 • Open 10am until late daily • $$*

Alto Cerro
The menu features home-reared geese, guinea fowl, rabbits, and turkeys, and fresh fruits *(see p132)*. ◈ *Map C3 • East of Constanza heading to Colonia Kennedy • 809 530 6192 • Open 8am–10pm daily • $$*

Rancho Camp David
Stunning views and high-class food make this the perfect place for a romantic dinner for two *(see p56)*.

Aroma de la Montaña
Located on top of a mountain outside Jarabacoa, this picture-perfect establishment combines stunning views with impressive food and great service. Probably the best place in the country to watch the sun set *(see p57)*.

Left **Costambar Beach** Right **Paradise Resort, Puerto Plata**

The Amber Coast

THE COSTA DE AMBAR, *named after the valuable resin to be found in the mountains inland, used to be the traditional center of the Dominican tourism industry, though now surpassed by Punta Cana/Bávaro. Visitors have been coming here since the 1970s, and large purpose-built resorts such as Playa Dorada meet their every need. But there is another dimension to this 200-mile (322-km) vista of sand and mountain, not least in the historical and cultural interest to be found in the 16th-century port city of Puerto Plata, where ancient fortifications and opulent fin de siècle mansions testify to its past. The action-packed beaches of Cabarete and Playa Grande are a magnet for surfers and independent travelers alike. In contrast are the calm and beckoning waters at places such as Sosúa and Playa Dorada.*

San Felipe Fortress, Puerto Plata

🔟 Sights

1. Puerto Plata
2. Costambar
3. Cofresí
4. Playa Dorada
5. Sosúa
6. Cabarete
7. Río San Juan
8. Playa Grande
9. Playa Caletón
10. Laguna Gri Gri

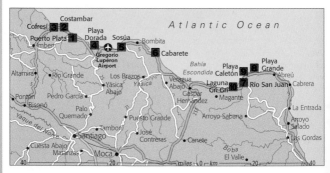

1 Puerto Plata

The biggest town on the North Coast with a long and interesting history, Puerto Plata is sometimes overlooked by visitors in their all-inclusive resorts. This is a shame, because this bustling place has much to offer: not only historic sites but also a range of atmospheric bars and restaurants. The San Felipe Fortress is certainly worth a visit, as is the charming Parque Central, but the highlight is the amazing cable car ride to the top of Pico Isabel de Torres, the lofty mountain that looks over the city and ocean *(see pp16–17)*.

2 Costambar

Only a short taxi ride away from the busy center of Puerto Plata, the beach is just west of town, offering a complete change of atmosphere from the city itself and from the highly developed tourist strip to the east at Playa Dorada. There are no big hotels here, but rather a cluster of tasteful waterfront villas and condominiums, mostly owned by well-heeled locals or foreigners. The beach itself is an extensive strip of soft white sand with calm water and very safe swimming. There is an array of restaurants and bars under the shade of the sea grape and palm trees that line the beach. ✪ *Map C1*

3 Cofresí

The advent of the Ocean World theme park in the vicinity of this formerly quiet fishing village, allegedly named after an infamous local pirate, has done much to change its ambience. But the delightfully curved horseshoe cove still draws many visitors to its generous expanse of sand and shade-giving trees. Expensive-looking villas gaze

Playa Dorada

down from the hillsides, while behind the beach stands the upmarket Lifestyle Hacienda Resort. The beach becomes much busier at weekends, when the surfing crowd comes in search of its hefty tides, but during the week you're likely to be much more on your own. ✪ *Map C1*
• *Lifestyle Hacienda Resort: 809 970 7777*

4 Playa Dorada

This tourist paradise used to have more than a dozen separate resorts, offering every conceivable activity and self-indulgence known to mankind. However, many have closed down due to a fall in tourist numbers. Nevertheless, it still provides a value-for-money holiday with a range of beach activities, which encompass everything from snorkeling to volleyball, while round-the-clock catering provides all sorts of eating and drinking options. The beach itself is a wonderfully white strip of soft sand, which is cleaned daily. The other most prized asset is the Robert Trent Jones-designed golf course. ✪ *Map C1* • *Playa Dorada Golf Club: Open 7am–7pm daily; 809 320 3472; Green fee & hire facilities*

Surfer at Cabarete Beach

Sosúa

Founded by Jewish refugees in 1940, Sosúa was later transformed from a small agricultural village where mainly German was spoken to a pulsating, international tourist venue. The place developed a rather unsavory reputation in the 1990s for the worst excesses of tourism, but has been cleaned up since and now offers a great mixture of nightlife and lazy days on the beach. Divided by the beach and bay into two separate and different *barrios*, Sosúa has a distinct tourist area called El Batey, where streets are lined with cafés and stores, and the more authentically Dominican district of Los Charamicos. ✎ *Map D1*

Cabarete

The first French Canadian windsurfers arrived in 1984, creating a surfing paradise around the long strip known as Playa Cabarete and a couple of nearby beaches. As a result, a modern tourist town has grown up between beach and lagoon, catering not only to the surfing fraternity but also to a growing range of independent travelers. Surfing, both windsurfing and increasingly kitesurfing, are Cabarete's main *raison d'être*, but there are many other activities on offer. ✎ *Map D1*

Río San Juan

A left turn off the coastal Carretera 5 takes you into the small and still unspoilt village of Río San Juan, once an isolated rural outpost but now firmly on the tourist map. There's still a working fisherman's harbor, and the gridiron Barrio Acapulco is filled with boats and other fishing paraphernalia. The village's beach is pretty but very small, so most visitors tend to head farther east down the coast. Rio San Juan's relaxed and friendly atmosphere can be easily sampled in the cafés and restaurants that line the central Calle Duarte. ✎ *Map E1*

Playa Grande, Río San Juan

A long stretch of perfect golden-hued sand, bordered by forest and demarcated by high cliffs, Playa Grande is unsurprisingly attracting a good deal of tourist development after years of isolation. A spectacular oceanside 18-hole golf course has already been built. The sea here is known for its waves and is more suitable for surfing than swimming, but at weekends the beach becomes very busy, especially at the end nearer Río San Juan, where food and drink are on sale. ✎ *Map E1*

Jewish Exiles

In 1940 several hundred Jewish refugees from Europe settled in Sosúa at the invitation of Trujillo, starting a dairy and smoked-meat industry that is still going strong. Now largely dispersed, the Jewish community's history can be explored in the small museum adjacent to the synagogue in El Batey.

---

9 Playa Caletón

A perfect cove of white sand with mangrove forest surrounding it, this is one of the most beautiful beaches on the North Coast. Even so, it is still not overcrowded yet, and on a week day visitors are liable to be few and far between. At weekends there are more locals around, and you can buy fried fish on the beach. Protected by two rocky and forest-clad promontories, the small bay, known locally by the diminutive La Playita, has shallow clean water, ideal for children. Ⓢ *Map E1*

10 Laguna Gri Gri

The mangrove-lined lagoon comes almost into the center of Río San Juan, and boat trips start from a jetty at the northern end of Calle Duarte. Tours take about two hours and pass through the mysterious lagoon landscape. There are crocodiles in the lagoon and a profusion of birdlife, encouraged by the area's environmentally protected status. The Cueva de las Golondrinas (Swallows' Cave), a subterranean passage formed by an earthquake, is home to countless birds, and there are more caves along the Atlantic shoreline. Ⓢ *Map E1 • Laguna Gri Gri tour office: Calle Duarte, Rio San Juan: 809 589 2277*

Boats at Laguna Gri Gri

Exploring Puerto Plata

🕐 Half a day is enough to see the main sights of this historically significant town, though if you wish to visit the **Brugal Rum Factory** (see p17) more time will be needed. Start in the morning in the **Parque Central** (also known as Parque Independencia), where you will see the attractive gazebo and fine Art Deco cathedral. It is worth bearing in mind that hiring a guide may produce some interesting information. Take a look at some of the restored 19th-century gingerbread-style houses in the old streets around the square.

Heading towards the sea, you'll reach the **Malecón** (see p16), the long waterside boulevard. Turn left from here to reach the promontory where the much patched-up but impressive Fortaleza de San Felipe stands guard over the harbor entrance. After inspecting the small museum, walk back to the Malecón, where there are plenty of bars and stalls selling cold drinks and snacks. Alternatively, stroll back to Calle 12 de Julio to visit the **Gregorio Luperon Museum** and have an iced coffee in the café there (see p16).

From here it's a fair way to the cable car installation that takes you to the top of the **Pico Isabel de Torres** (see p17), so it is worth taking a taxi. The 20-minute ascent over dense tropical vegetation and the view from the top are breathtaking. At the peak is a pleasant botanic garden and a cafeteria, suitable for a light lunch.

Left **Casa Veintiuno, Sosúa** Right **Rocky's Rock and Blues Bar, Sosúa**

10 Places to Eat & Drink

1 Kilometro Zero
This friendly restaurant and sports bar serves up a wide range of Italian and international food. ⊛ *Map C1 • Avenida Ginebra 6, Puerto Plata • 809 244 4346 • Open 10am–midnight. Closed Wed • $$$*

2 Casa Colonial
An upscale restaurant in a boutique hotel, offering Caribbean-fusion fare and incredible views of the mangrove jungle. ⊛ *Map C1 • Playa Dorada, Puerto Plata • 809 320 3232 • Open 7pm–10pm • $$$$$*

Casa del Pescador, Cabarete

3 Green Jack
Sit inside or out to enjoy the exceptional Caribbean cuisine at this beachfront eatery. ⊛ *Map C1 • Blue Jack Tar hotel, Playa Dorada, Puerto Plata • 809 320 3800 • Open noon–11pm Sun–Thu, noon–midnight Fri & Sat • $$$$*

4 Chez Arsenio
Traditional, thatched-roof restaurant on the beach with an international menu, great desserts, and attentive staff. ⊛ *Map D1 • Hideaway beach, Carreterra Sosúa-Cabarete • 809 571 9948 • Open 11am–10pm Mon–Fri, 9am–10pm Sat & Sun • $$$*

5 Morua Mai
Choose from a varied menu that includes pizza, imported meat, fresh fish, and seafood. ⊛ *Map D1 • Calle Pedro Clisante, Sosúa • 809 571 2503 • Open 8am–midnight • $$$$*

6 Rocky's Rock and Blues Bar
A great place to hang out and enjoy an American-style menu that includes subs, sandwiches, ribs, kebabs, and more. ⊛ *Map D1 • Calle Dr Rosen 24, Sosúa • 809 571 2951 • Open 8am until late daily • $$*

7 Casa Veintiuno
A stylish international restaurant with an extensive menu and a great wine list. ⊛ *Map D1 • Calle Piano 1, Tavares, Sosúa • 829 342 8089 • Open 6pm–11pm Wed–Sun • $$$$*

8 Las Palmas
Located in an elegant house, this restaurant offers great service and excellent Italian cuisine. ⊛ *Map C1 • Calle Luis Ginebra 47, Puerto Plata • 809 586 7065 • Open noon–11pm daily • $$$*

9 Casa del Pescador
Restaurant in a lovely beach position, with waves lapping close by. Specializes in fish and seafood. ⊛ *Map D1 • Cabarete Beach • 809 571 0760 • Open 11am–11pm daily • $$*

10 Diego's Restaurant
Situated in Hotel Catalina, with views of lush gardens and the ocean, Diego's offers local organic produce and an extensive wine list. ⊛ *Map E1 • Bahía Blanca, Los Farallones, Cabrera • 809 589 7700 • Open for lunch & dinner • $$$*

Price Categories

Price categories include a three-course meal for one, a beer and all unavoidable extra charges including tax.

$	under US$10
$$	US$10–US$20
$$$	US$20–US$30
$$$$	US$30–US$40
$$$$$	over US$40

José Oshay's Irish Beach Pub, Cabarete

🔟 Nightlife

1 Havana Club
A beach bar and a disco, this place gets extremely lively after midnight. ◈ Map D1
• Cabarete • Open 11am until late

2 Onno's
A hot nightspot with great music, and dancing that goes on into the early hours. There is a resident international karaoke DJ.
◈ Map D1 • Cabarete • Open 11am–6am

3 Lax Ojo
A popular restaurant by day, this bistro-cum-bar becomes a two-story discotheque at night. It is the perfect venue for beach parties. ◈ Map D1 • Cabarete • Open 9am–1am

4 Coco Bongo
One of the most frequented discos in Playa Dorada, Coco Bongo offers typical Dominican and international dance music (see p61).

5 Bar El General
A trendy and sophisticated cocktail bar, with beer on tap, great music and plenty of dancing. Often offers special promotions.
◈ Map D1 • Alejo Martinez, Sosúa
• Open 4pm–1:30am daily

6 Rumba Bar
This restaurant and bar has a great terrace and late-night dancing. A popular joint that remains packed every night.
◈ Map D1 • Calle Pedro Clisante, Sosúa
• Open noon until late

7 D'Classico-Club 59
One of the leading night spots in Sosúa, drawing crowds from all over the North Coast, especially unattached males. DJs play a mix of Latin and international music. At weekends, it's mainly Dominican music (see p61).

8 After One
When other pubs close, this place comes alive, playing hip-hop, rap, and electronic music, plus salsa, merengue, and bachata. ◈ Map D1 • In front of Hotel Sosúa Bay • Open 1–4am

9 Playa Chiquita Casino
This casino offers blackjack, roulette, poker, and slot machines, as well as private rooms. ◈ Map D1
• Avenida Martinez, Sosúa • Open 8pm–4am Mon–Thu, 4pm–4am Fri & Sat

10 José Oshay's Irish Beach Pub
A popular beachfront bar featuring occasional live music performances. It also has a large screen for all major sporting events (see p58).

Bar El General, Sosúa

➤ Following pages **Victorian house in Puerto Plata**

91

Left **French clock tower, Monte Cristi** Center **El Morro, Parque Nacional** Right **Playa Ensenada**

The Northwest

L ITTLE HAS CHANGED IN THIS *isolated and unexplored area of the country. There are hardly any tourist resorts as yet, and time seems to have stopped still in the sleepy towns and villages that dot the empty landscape. A mix of small farms and bone-dry desert wilderness, the region has little of the lushness to be found elsewhere, suggesting that life here is often hard. Yet, despite the sometimes-forbidding appearance of the terrain, the Northwest has distinct attractions, not least its fascinating ecosystems, best explored in the Parque Nacional Monte Cristi. Its beaches, too, are magnificent, and, because of its out-of-the-way character, less developed than those to the east of Puerto Plata.*

Mangroves, Parque Nacional Monte Cristi

Sights

1. Monte Cristi
2. Parque Nacional Monte Cristi
3. Cayos de los Siete Hermanos
4. Playa Ensenada
5. La Isabela
6. Luperón
7. Puerto Blanco Marina
8. Playa Grande
9. Manzanillo
10. Dajabón

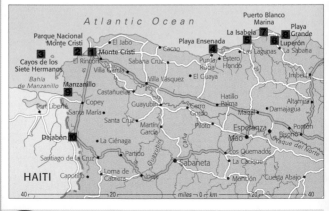

Monte Cristi

Like some cowboy movie set, the main town of the region has a rather melancholic feel, and is in the scorchingly hot and flat delta of the Río Yaque del

Cactus, Parque Nacional

Norte. Monte Cristi was once an important port, exporting tobacco and mahogany. The Victorian buildings situated around the Parque Central give an idea of its golden age, which came to an end when a railway link from Santiago to Puerto Plata supplanted it. The French clock tower and various ginger-bread mansions are worth a look, especially the ornate Villa Doña Emilia Jiménez. ◈ Map A1

Parque Nacional Monte Cristi

Divided between a series of offshore islands, a mangrove delta, and a large inland expanse of desert badlands, the national park shelters a profusion of wildlife, including crocodiles, turtles, and innumerable bird species. The most accessible and interesting part is the flat-topped mountain of El Morro, the imposing outcrop that looks like a sleeping camel. You can walk up some steps from the

national park office through a cleavage in the mountain, reaching an isolated beach below, from where it's a relatively short swim to Isla Cabrita. The sea around Monte Cristi is said to be full of shipwrecks (see p40).

Cayos de los Siete Hermanos

The "Seven Brothers" are a cluster of tiny islets or cays, flat and dry, lying within the Parque Nacional Monte Cristi. Almost entirely devoid of vegetation, these arid sand spits are surrounded by some of the most pristine reefs in the Caribbean, rarely visited by divers. The islands are a haven for seabirds and turtles, which have always used them as egg-laying territory, but it is reported that poaching is now a major problem. Excursions by boat to the cays can be organized, either from a hotel or from the beach of Playa Juan de Bolaños. ◈ Map A1

Playa Ensenada

This stretch of fine white sand shares a headland with the Punta Rucia Beach (see p19) to the west, which is easily accessible from the small village of Estero Hondo. It is one of the best beaches in the country, with clear, shallow waters and mountain views. Beach shacks line the coast here, all serving fresh fish, lobster, and seafood snacks. Sit on the chairs provided and soak up the scenery. Scenic boat trips can also be taken from here to Cayo Paraíso. The beach gets extremely busy at weekends, so arrive early to claim your spot. ◈ Map B1

Isla Cabrita, Monte Cristi

Puerto Blanco Marina, Luperón

5 La Isabela

The site of Columbus's first permanent settlement in the Americas is full of historic interest and natural beauty. Looking out over the Atlantic Ocean, the bluff where the explorer established a European toehold contains the foundations of a warehouse, chapel, and rudimentary hospital. The Parque Nacional La Isabela museum explains the site's significance, while the cemetery nearby is an atmospheric patch of tombstones and acacia trees *(see pp18–19)*. ◈ *Map B1*
• *Parque Nacional Histórico La Isabela: open 8am–6pm Mon–Sat • Adm*

6 Luperón

Named after a Puerto Plata tobacco magnate, military leader, and president, this small town is typical of the Northwest. It offers little in the way of conventional tourist attractions, but boasts rural atmosphere. The Parque Central is the focal point, with most of the local fish restaurants and bars. Luperón's main claim to fame, however, is its natural bay, which is a favorite with the yachting fraternity. ◈ *Map C1*

7 Puerto Blanco Marina

This magnet for yachties, 2 miles (3.2 km) out of Luperón village, draws a good number of visitors. The marina is located in the estuary, framed by mangrove

forests and sheltering hills, with boats moored in the calm anchorage. The bar and restaurant are normally busy, and non-sailors are always welcome. From here it's easy to take a catamaran tour of the estuary and the coast, find a boat to Cayo Paraíso, and to hire diving and snorkeling equipment. With its cosmopolitan crowd of sailing aficionados, the marina has a different feel to the rest of the region. ◈ *Map C1*

8 Playa Grande

Not to be confused with the magnificent beach of the same name near Río San Juan, this more modest stretch of sand is Luperón's local seaside attraction. The sea here is inviting, the row of palm trees provides welcome shade, and

Parque Nacional La Isabela

Dominican Freedom Fighter

One house on Monte Cristi's main square with special historic significance is that formerly owned by Máximo Gómez, the Dominican-born fighter for Cuban independence. Now a museum, it was here that he signed the famous independence declaration along with José Martí before setting off to fight the Spanish colonialists in Cuba.

Manzanillo

the sand is pleasantly soft and clean. Nearby are a handful of bars and eating places.
🛇 *Map C1*

9 Manzanillo

The border town and port of Manzanillo, also known since the 1930s as Pepillo Salcedo, is as isolated a spot as you're likely to find in the Dominican Republic. But it's interesting because of its proximity to Haiti and its history as a major banana-exporting center and dock. Nowadays, the port looks very run-down, but there are plans afoot to erect a new industrial complex. From the town itself, you can look over the Massacre River into Haitian territory, but there's no official crossing point here. The nearby lagoon and salt marsh shelters hosts of flamingos and other waders. 🛇 *Map A1*

10 Dajabón

One of two official crossing points with neighboring Haiti, the town is famous for its Monday and Friday markets. Crowds of Haitian vendors cross the bridge over the dividing river and set up stalls near the crossing. The resulting hubbub of commercial transactions is loud and colorful, as Haitians and Dominicans haggle furiously over basics. The market is usually over by mid-afternoon, so it's worth arriving early to see the action and maybe snap up a bargain or two. 🛇 *Map A2*

From Puerto Plata to La Isabela & Back

Morning

🕐 Leave **Puerto Plata** *(see pp16–17)* early, heading south towards **Santiago** *(see pp14–15)* on the Carretera 5. After about 6 miles (10 km) take a right turn onto a road signposted RIO Resorts. This rough but passable route takes you through some beautiful rural scenery, including **Maimón Beach** and a series of tiny fishing and farming villages. Keep your eyes firmly on the road, as there are many animals.

💻 The road comes out at **La Sabana**. A right from here leads to **Luperón**. You can stop here for a drink, or pass through town and stop by **Puerto Blanco Marina** for refreshments.

Another 8 miles (13 km) or so along the Carretera de las Américas through dry woodland and flocks of goats, brings you to the pretty seaside village of **El Castillo**. Just before the village entrance is the turn-off for the **Parque Nacional La Isabela**. An hour or so is sufficient time to look around.

🍴 At lunchtime, go into **El Castillo**. Near **Rancho del Sol** hotel on the right there are several good Dominican *comedors* to try for lunch. Or head back to the marina or **Luperón's Playa Grande** for food.

Afternoon

Returning to **Puerto Plata**, it's quicker, if less scenic, to go straight to the major junction of **Imbert**, where the Texaco garage marks the road back.

➡️ *Many hotels offer excursions to the market at Dajabón; Caribe Tour buses also go there*

Left **Mangroves, Parque Nacional Monte Cristi** Right **Orchids**

TOP10 Wildlife

1 Mangroves
The gnarled thickets of vegetation, their roots emerging from mudflats, estuaries, and lagoons, are a unique ecosystem, providing food and shelter to a huge spectrum of birds, fish, and crustaceans.

2 Crocodiles
Like their relatives in Lago Enriquillo *(see pp26–7)*, the Northwest's American crocodiles are not remotely aggressive, fleeing approaching humans and thriving on fish. Their preferred habitat is mangrove forests.

3 Turtles
The offshore cays are favored breeding grounds for the giant leatherback, loggerhead, and small green turtles. They lay large quantities of eggs on the beaches of these desert islands.

4 Pelicans
The huge, heavy brown pelican, with long bill and pouch, can be seen either swimming in the sea or diving spectacularly at a steep angle in search of a fish.

5 Ibises
The gregarious ibises, white with a trademark red bill and face, roost and feed in large flocks. They prefer mudflats and shallow lagoons, where they love to feed on crabs and small fish.

6 Oystercatchers
The American oystercatcher is difficult to confuse with any of the other waders due to its large size, striking black and white plumage, and bright orange bill.

7 Egrets
Taller and whiter than the cattle egret, the snowy egret is another mangrove-loving bird. It nests in colonies in the protective thickets and stalks its prey in the shallow waters *(see p67)*.

8 Orchids
Hundreds of species of orchid of every color abound in the swamps of the Parque Nacional Monte Cristi *(see pp40 & 95)*. Some grow out of trees, the others mysteriously thrive on dry rock faces *(see p64)*.

9 Cacti
The region's desert conditions are ideal for many different sorts of cactus. The best-loved, though, is called *tuna*, the prickly pear, which boasts lovely white flowers and bears edible fruit.

10 Mosquitoes
Obviously, the least-loved of natural inhabitants, these irritating creatures proliferate in the swampy conditions. They can create a genuine health hazard, and cases of dengue fever exist throughout the country. Malaria has been reported near Haiti *(see p116)*.

Ibis

Left **Puerto Blanco Marina, Luperón** Right **Seafood platter**

Places to Eat & Drink

1 Tres Cocos
The delicious dishes made by the European chef here come highly recommended. The meat and seafood dishes are particularly good. ◈ *Map C1 • Las Rocas, Cofresí • 809 970 7627 • Open 11am–11pm • $$$$*

2 Le Papillon
One of the best places to eat outside the all-inclusive hotels, this fine international restaurant is German-owned and specializes in steaks. ◈ *Map C1 • Villas Cofresí, just east of Ocean World • 809 970 7640 • Open 6–10pm Tue–Sun • $$$$$*

3 Ahora Beach House
This restaurant is famous in the region for its typical Dominican cuisine and *puerco asado* dishes on weekends (pork roasted over an open fire). Also offers Mexican and international dishes. ◈ *Map C1 • Calle Principal, Playa Cofresí • 809 881 0874 • Open 10am–11pm • $$$$*

4 Puerto Blanco Marina
Dine in the pretty setting of a lagoon surrounded by mangroves. Enjoy seafood at the restaurant and live music at the popular bar. ◈ *Map C1 • Luperón • 809 707 2629 • Open 8am–11pm • $$$*

5 Letty
This bistro is famous for its authentic Dominican fare and delicious seafood. In the evenings and at weekends, it is packed with locals dining alfresco. ◈ *Map C1 • 27 de Febrero 46, Luperón • Open 8am–11pm • $–$$*

6 La Yola
This German-owned eatery near the marina has tasty seafood as well as international cuisine. ◈ *Map C1 • 27 de Febrero 69, Luperón • 809 571 8511 • Open 3–11pm Sat & Sun • $$*

7 Don Gaspar
A hotel and restaurant, Don Gaspar specializes in Dominican and Spanish dishes. Try the eggs and *mangú*, mashed plantain with onions. ◈ *Map A1 • Pte Jiménez 21 esquina Rodríguez Camargo, Monte Cristi • 809 579 2477 • Open 8am–10pm • $–$$*

8 El Bistrot
A charming restaurant set in a colonial courtyard. Its elegant bar and extensive menu of seafood, salads, and pasta make it very popular. ◈ *Map A1 • San Fernando 26, Monte Cristi • 809 579 2091 • Open noon–2:30pm, 6–10pm • $$*

9 Putulas Parilla
Sip cocktails and devour tasty fresh fish and barbecue dinners at this open-air, thatched-roof bar and restaurant. Dinner reservation recommended. ◈ *Map C1 • Luperón • Open 10am–10pm, Food available 10am–8pm • $$$*

10 Cocomar
Tasty food at reasonable prices, although the paella and the seafood platter are a little more costly. ◈ *Map A1 • Calle Juan de Bolaño 2, Monte Cristi • 809 579 3354 • Open 9am–11pm • $$*

Around the Dominican Republic – The Northwest

Samaná Bay footbridge and sailboats

The Samaná Peninsula

JUTTING OUT INTO THE ATLANTIC OCEAN, *the Samaná Peninsula is a strip of mountainous and verdant land, where the sea is never far away. Water is omnipresent, with views of the sea at every turn, but also in the form of fresh-water streams and cascading waterfalls. Combined with above-average rainfall, this environment produces a spectacle of densely wooded hillsides and coconut groves. Perhaps due to the late arrival of a non-intensive form of tourism, it is more relaxed than elsewhere. History, too, seems to have given it a separate identity. There are stronger traces of a Taíno heritage in these parts, and in and around Samaná town are the descendants of English-speaking African-Americans who moved here in the 1820s.*

Left **Samaná harbor** Right **Windsurfer, Samaná Bay**

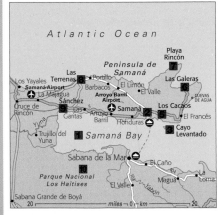

Sights

1 Samaná Bay
2 Samaná
3 Cayo Levantado
4 Whale-Watching
5 Los Cacaos
6 Las Galeras
7 Playa Rincón
8 Las Terrenas
9 Sánchez
10 Parque Nacional
   Los Haïtises

1 Samaná Bay

The vast, glittering expanse of Samaná Bay comes into view as you drive along the Peninsula's southern coast road. This magnificent natural harbor, sheltered by surrounding hills, forms a perfect haven from hurricanes. In the 19th and early 20th centuries, several European powers as well as the US saw the Bay's potential as a naval base. Luckily, the plans never materialized, and the bay remains largely unspoilt, with beautiful beaches, seaside villages, and fantastic views across the placid water. The bay attracts not just sailors and devotees of water sports, but also humpback whales, which mate and raise their young here. ✎ Map F3

2 Samaná

Santa Bárbara de Samaná is the main town on the Peninsula, a busy little port overlooking the huge bay. While much less of an obvious tourist destination than Las Terrenas (see pp20–21), it has plenty of charm, despite the fact that most of its Victorian-era architecture was demolished in an ill-advised 1970s modernization scheme. The mostly concrete buildings are laid out in a grid system. The focal point is the wide seaside Malecón (boulevard) – a magnet for those who enjoy a walk, especially in the evening. Look out, too, for La Churcha (see p49). ✎ Map F2

3 Cayo Levantado

A stunningly pretty desert island, Cayo Levantado lies a couple of miles offshore from Samaná and is easily reached by regular

Malecón, Samaná

boat services from the Malecón. Dubbed "Bacardi Island," the tropical charm of this Robinson Crusoe-style cay is such that it's said that a famous 1970s Bacardi commercial, featuring white sands and a particularly pretty palm tree, was filmed here. Nowadays, it's advisable to arrive early or visit later in the day, as the island can be very crowded with excursionists around lunchtime. Some areas of the island are reserved for the use of guests of local luxury hotels. ✎ Map F3

4 Whale-Watching

The whale-watching season around Samaná generally lasts from January to March, when an estimated 6,000 humpback whales – the whole population of the North Atlantic – converge on the waters around the Peninsula. The mating and rearing activity takes place in Banca de Plata (Silver Bank) to the north of the Peninsula, and in and around the bay itself, where the shallow and warm water is conducive to courtship displays as well as birthing. Humpback whales can weigh up to 40 tons, so their acrobatics of diving, rolling, and leaping clean out of the water are spectacular.

Malecón, Samaná

➡ Public ferries operate daily from Malecón to the island of Cayo Levantado at US$7 each way

Playa Bonita, Las Terrenas

Los Cacaos

The road eastwards out of Samaná runs along the shoreline, passing numerous beaches. At the small village of Los Cacaos you'll discover a truly wonderful hotel, the Gran Bahía Principe (see p133). Los Cacaos village itself is a modest fishing community, with no tourist facilities. But a rough track up into the mountains leads to an impressive waterfall, with plentiful cold water rushing down the green hillside. Map F2

Las Galeras

Lying at the eastern extreme of the Samaná Peninsula, the charming village of Las Galeras has witnessed significant tourist development over the last two decades. But it has not yet lost the ambience of a remote and relaxed fishing community. The main attraction is the beach, a strip of fine sand set in a pretty curving bay backed by cliffs and forested hillsides. Unspoiled by commercial sprawl and hustling, this is a beautiful place, with its calm, shallow, and inviting water. A smattering of hotels, guesthouses, and restaurants offers a choice of accommodation and eating options. Map F2

Playa Rincón

Drive from Las Galeras or take a scenic 20-minute boat ride to the splendidly isolated and spectacular Playa Rincón, hidden by the steep bluffs at each end of the beach. Aficionados claim that this is the best beach on the Peninsula, and it's easy to see why. A 2-mile (3.2-km) stretch of bleached sand is bordered by azure sea and leads back inland to an expanse of coconut trees. While hardly a secret, its distance from the main resorts ensures this beach is relatively uncrowded compared to others in the Dominican Republic (see p44). Map F2

Las Terrenas

The most developed tourist spot on the Peninsula is a fairly relaxed place, where life revolves around a couple of beaches, seafood restaurants and a busy nightlife. Hotels and guesthouses are mostly small, and situated along the main town beach or the next-door Playa Bonita. A single main street is lined with stores, cafés, restaurants, and nearly all entertainment needs are catered to in town (see pp20–21). Map F2

Sánchez

Traditionally the gateway to the Samaná Peninsula, Sánchez is where all vehicles used to turn

---

Peninsula for Sale

The strategic significance of the Peninsula and Bay did not go unnoticed by various Dominican presidents in the 19th century, who tried to cash in on this asset. In 1868, President Cabral, for instance, offered the whole Peninsula to the US for a $1-million down payment and an annual rent of $300,000.

For further information on hotels along the Samaná Peninsula, log on to www.gosamana-dominicanrepublic.com

off to cross the mountains over to Las Terrenas, but the opening of the Atlantic Boulevard in 2011, has reduced the traffic. It was an important place when a rail connection linked the port to the agricultural powerhouse of the Cibao Valley. But those days are long gone, and now the town is going to seed, kept alive only by its fishing industry and the relatively small number of tourists that visit. The old times are visible in a handful of ornate but crumbling gingerbread-style mansions near the waterfront. ◈ *Map F2*

10 Parque Nacional Los Haïtises

Samaná is the most convenient starting point for a day trip to this wild nature reserve. A boat departs daily, crossing to the Sabana de la Mar fishing port, where hired guides can lead a boat trip to the small part of the park that's open to visitors. Here, you're confronted by one of the country's most unique landscapes: hump-shaped hillocks rising out of the water and covered with dense tropical vegetation. These strange *mogotes*, along with mangroves and rainforest, shelter a variety of flora and fauna. ◈ *Map E3*

Old Victorian house, Sánchez

From Samaná to Las Galeras

Morning

🕐 Leave **Samaná** after breakfast, heading eastwards along the Carretera 5. On the left are steep hillsides dotted with small farms and rural settlements, on the right the broad vista over the **Samaná Bay**.

Following **Playa Las Flechas**, a beach named after the arrows that local Taino tribesmen reportedly shot at Christopher Columbus on his first visit, is a small jetty and fishing village called **Simi Baez**. Here you can either take a ferry to the nearby **Cayo Levantado**, or spend some time on the beach or another nearby stretch of sand called **Anacaona**.

The road continues along the coast, revealing exuberant vegetation and idyllic bays, until at **Los Cacaos** you come across the Victorian elegance of the **Gran Bahía** resort, surrounded by colorful gardens. From here, turning northwards, the road passes through an unusual landscape of limestone caves, known as the **Cuevas de Agua**, where locals will be happy to show the subterranean **Taino sites**.

Afternoon

Aim to arrive in **Las Galeras** in time for lunch. Try the food at **El Marinique** *(see p104)*, which specializes in steaks and seafood, or at one of the other eateries around. Then it's time to visit the beach itself, choosing a shady spot – but not one directly under a cluster of coconuts.

Around the Dominican Republic – The Samaná Peninsula

For more information on Parque Nacional Los Haïtises, visit their office at Sabana de la Mar or call 809 556 7333

Left **Villa Serena, Las Galeras** Right **The Beach Restaurant, Las Terrenas**

🔟 Places to Eat & Drink

1 Bambú
Dine on a pleasant terrace with views over the harbor at Bambú. On the menu is a local specialty, *pescado al coco* (fish in coconut sauce). ✆ *Map F2 • Av Malecón, Ed. 3, Samaná • 809 923 6539 • Open 11am–10pm daily • $$$*

2 La Dolce Vita
Excellent Italian food at an enviable location on Punta Popy beach. A magnet for expats and visitors. ✆ *Map F2 • Punta Popy, Las Terrenas • 809 989 5766 • Open noon–10pm daily • $$$*

3 Chez Denise
Colorful decor and friendly service makes this a popular stop for snacks as well as meals. Don't miss the delicious crêpes with a variety of fillings, the tasty shrimps, or the salads. ✆ *Map F2 • Calle Principal, Las Galeras • 809 538 0219 • Open 9am–10pm daily • $$*

4 Il Pirata
Owner Manuela serves tasty Italian dishes using fresh ingredients, followed by home-made ice cream. The seafood is especially recommended. ✆ *Map F2 • Calle Principal, Plaza Lusitania, Las Galeras • 809 538 0093 • Open noon–11pm daily • $$*

5 Villa Serena
Gourmet dining and delightful views of the hotel garden's abundant flowers and palm trees. Open for breakfast, lunch, and dinner *(see p133).*

6 El Marinique
An open-air seaside restaurant serving terrific food – notably papaya crêpes with maple syrup, and mouthwatering pizza. ✆ *Map F2 • Las Galeras • 809 538 0262 • Open for breakfast, lunch, & dinner • $$$$*

7 Restaurant Luis
Located on beautiful Playa Coson beach, this typical Dominican shack is very popular with locals and expats alike for its fabulous seafood. The piña coladas are to die for. ✆ *Map E2 • Playa Coson, Las Terrenas • Open 11am–8pm daily • $–$$*

8 The Beach Restaurant
This eatery is beautiful in every way, located in the upmarket Victorian-era Peninsula House hotel, serving fresh Caribbean food amid beautiful surroundings on the beach. ✆ *Map E2 • Playa Coson, Las Terrenas • 809 962 7447 • Open for lunch only noon–3pm. Closed Mon • $$$*

9 La Terrasse
Located in the Fisherman's Village, La Terrasse serves great French fare, and has an excellent wine list. The *steak au poivre* is superb. ✆ *Map F2 • Pueblo de los Pescadores, Las Terrenas • 809 240 6730 • Open 11:30am–2:30pm, 6:30–11pm daily. Dinner only in low season. • $$*

10 El Paraíso
A beach bar offering refreshing drinks, delectable fish, and shrimp, baked or fried. ✆ *Map F2 • El Paraíso, Playa El Valle • Open 11am–6pm daily • $$*

Pueblo Principe, Samaná

⅒ Clubs & Bars

1 Mojitos

One of the most famous bars in the area, Mojitos serves a mix of Cuban and Dominican food and, of course, fabulous mojitos. ⊗ *Map F2 • Punta Popi, Las Terrenas • Open 8am–8pm daily*

2 XO Brasserie

This upscale club, situated on the beach with stunning views, is elegantly fitted out, and serves a choice of tapas or light meals for peckish clientele. ⊗ *Map F2 • Avenida Libertad 3, Las Terrenas • 809 816 3266• Open 6pm–2am daily*

3 La Bodega

You can dance to merengue and Latin music at this bar and dance floor on the patio of Casa Linda. There's sometimes live music. ⊗ *Map F2 • Av 27 de Febrero (in front of cemetery), Las Terrenas • Open 6pm until late*

4 El Balconcito

This great bar is on a quiet stretch of beach just outside town. Put your feet in the sand and watch the sun go down while enjoying one of the many cocktails from the impressive list. ⊗ *Map F2 • Carretera El Limon • 809-877-2844 • Open 11am until late*

5 Barrio Latino

Primarily a restaurant, Barrio Latino is also a swinging bar that stays open until midnight. ⊗ *Map F2 • Paseo de la Costanera, Las Terrenas • 809 240 6367 • Open 8am–11pm Mon–Sat*

6 Clandestino Bar

This popular and intimate two-story bar in the Fisherman's Village has a small dance floor and a lovely outdoor terrace. Always lively and full of people. ⊗ *Map F2 • Pueblo de los Pescadores • 809 703 2114 • Open 6pm–4am daily*

7 One Love Surf Shack

Canadian-owned sports bar, with a big screen and Bob Marley pictures on the wall. Live music attracts many, as do the tasty North American bites. ⊗ *Map F2 • Pueblo de los Pescadores, Las Terrenas • 809 655 9549 • Open 10am until late*

8 Pueblo Principe

In this purpose-built Caribbean-style village you can enjoy a traditional piano bar or a disco. There's also a large screen showing sports events. ⊗ *Map F2 • Malecón, Samaná • Open 10am until late*

9 Malecón, Samána

During weekends and fiestas this boulevard springs into action at night, when bars and stalls serving beer and rum appear along its length. ⊗ *Map F2 • Samaná*

10 Club Gaia

This three-story nightclub offers a different ambience at each level. The first floor is dominated by Latin sounds, the second focuses on house music, and the third, which is the roof, plays host to a chill-out zone. ⊗ *Map F2 • Pueblo de los Pescadores, Las Terrenas • 809 240 5133 • Open 10pm until late*

Around the Dominican Republic – The Samaná Peninsula

Following pages **Children playing on Barahona Beach**

Left **Hotel Las Salinas, Las Salinas** Right **Azua**

The Southwest

A LARGE SWATHE OF TERRITORY EXTENDS *down from the western outskirts of Santo Domingo to the Haitian border, incorporating some of the country's most diverse and dramatic landscapes. The coastline contains a variety of beaches, ranging from remote and undeveloped coves to crowded weekend favorites. Inland, lush, irrigated farmland stands in stark contrast to some of the country's driest desert terrain. Historic towns and cities dot this corner of the Dominican Republic, but its real appeal lies in its natural grandeur. The Sierra de Baoruco is an almost untouched wilderness of mountain rainforest; the Lago Enriquillo, famous for its crocodiles, is better known, but is isolated enough to inspire awe. Tourism has yet to change the character of this region, where the proximity of Haiti is keenly felt, but it's only a matter of time.*

Salt and water transportation system, Las Salinas

🔟 Sights

1. San Cristóbal
2. Baní
3. Las Salinas
4. Azua
5. Barahona
6. Lago Enriquillo
7. Laguna Rincón
8. Sierra de Baoruco
9. Pedernales
10. Parque Nacional Jaragua

➡ *The coast road from Barahona to Juancho is said to be the most spectacular road in the Caribbean*

The cathedral, San Cristóbal

San Cristóbal
Birthplace of the dictator Trujillo *(see p31)*, this busy provincial center received a great deal of public money during his 30-year regime. It resulted in the construction of an impressive cathedral and surrounding public buildings as well as two nearby residences for Trujillo. The cathedral is certainly worth a visit in order to view the dictator's ornate tomb, which was never used. More interesting are the caves at El Pomier *(see p32)* and the beaches at Palenque and Najayo, to the south of San Cristóbal. ✎ *Map D4*

Baní
Set among flat sugarcane-producing land, Baní is an industrious place, its relative wealth due to nearby coffee plantations, salt mining, and commerce. It is also renowned nationally for its particularly delicious mangoes, in season from May to July. Its most famous son is Máximo Gómez *(see p96)*, who with José Martí was the foremost champion of Cuban independence. A park containing his statue can be reached on foot from the pleasant Parque Central. Also worth a look is Baní's local beach, Los Almendros,

Máximo Gómez, Baní

with rough sand but with restaurants and plenty of atmosphere at weekends. ✎ *Map D5*

Las Salinas
The small peninsula forming the southern edge of the Bahía de Las Calderas creates an attractive ecosystem, containing salt flats and the most extensive sand dunes in the Caribbean. A naval base is sited here, but visitors can drive through to reach the outpost of Las Salinas, where a hotel and restaurant caters to visitors. The working salt extraction plant is conspicuous through its huge white mountains of finished salt. But the most spectacular views are from the sandy hill-sides facing out to the Caribbean. ✎ *Map D5 • Hotel Las Salinas, Puerto Hermosa 7, Baní: 809 866 8141*

Azua
Swelteringly hot in the plains between sea and mountains, Azua de Compostela looks like an ordinary Dominican town, but it is one of the New World's oldest cities. It was founded in 1504 by Diego de Valásquez, who went on to conquer Cuba. The old colonial settlement was ravaged by war and earthquakes, and the town was rebuilt away from the sea. There are some pretty painted wooden houses at a distance from the main road, but most visitors and locals prefer to head for the Playa Monte Río, a quiet and undeveloped beach with fabulous views over the Bahía de Ocoa and surrounding mountains. ✎ *Map C4*

Barahona

5 The biggest town in the region, the port of Barahona is the gateway to the Southwest's natural attractions. A broad seaside boulevard runs the length of the town,

Children at Barahona Beach

and the narrow streets around the Parque Central have some nice old buildings. The advent of an international airport in the 1990s encouraged some tourist development, including a beachside resort in the town itself. However, few visitors confine themselves to Barahona, preferring to explore the coastline to the south and the two nearby national parks. ◈ *Map B5*

Lago Enriquillo

6 Probably the country's most intriguing natural phenomenon, this huge saltwater lake is eerily atmospheric in its spectacular natural setting. The lake also forms an inland ecosystem, with its mixture of saline water, ancient fossils, and varied wildlife. Chief among these are the American crocodiles that inhabit its main island, the Isla Cabritos *(see pp26–7)*. ◈ *Map A4*

Laguna Rincón

7 Filled with fresh rather than salt water, Laguna Rincón, near the village of Cabral, is another surprisingly large lake, the

American crocodiles at Lago Enriquillo

country's second biggest after Laguna Limón. You can get close to the water on the small road from Cabral which skirts the lake, but the best way is to take a guided boat trip *(see p26)*. The lagoon and surrounding land forms an officially protected Reserva Científica (Scientific Reserve) and is home to a colony of freshwater slider turtles, found only on the Hispaniola Island. ◈ *Map B5*

Sierra de Baoruco

8 A wild and rugged range of mountains that march westwards over the Haitian border, these impressive peaks make up the Dominican Republic's second highest sierra. It was in this impenetrable tangle of mountains, valleys, and forests that the Taino leader Enriquillo *(see p31)* assembled his rebel forces and held out for 14 years against the Spanish. Now designated a national park, the range is covered in dense pine forests and subtropical rainforest. There are few passable roads, but it's theoretically possible, with a sturdy jeep, to drive along the rough track from Pedernales to Aguacate. ◈ *Map A5*

Bateyes

The area around Barahona is dotted with so-called *bateyes*, barrack-like villages usually inhabited by Haitian cane-cutters, who work seasonally on the plantations. These settlements have been condemned over the years as squalid, but for many Haitians and Haitian-descended Dominicans they represent a real sense of community and, as a result, are slowly being improved.

9 Pedernales

Pedernales is quite literally the end of the track, the final Dominican outpost before crossing over into Haiti. This remote settlement of one-story concrete buildings huddled together, is hardly a conventional tourist destination. But the place is not without interest, especially on Mondays and Fridays when the no-man's-land between the two countries is the scene of a large open-air market. The village's beach is also worth a visit, and from here it's usually easy to walk over the border. ◈ *Map A5*

10 Parque Nacional Jaragua

The park comprises the most southerly tip of the country, the Pedernales Peninsula, as well as Isla Beata, an uninhabited scrub-covered island. At more than 500 sq miles (1,293 sq km), this is the biggest of the national parks, comprising dry limestone studded with cacti and other desert vegetation. This terrain is home to a huge array of land and sea birds, iguanas, lizards, and bats. The best way to get a sense of its natural importance is to contact the national park office near the village of Oviedo, for the boat tours of Laguna Oviedo. ◈ *Map A6 • Open 9am–5pm daily • Adm*

Fishermen holding starfish, Pedernales

Day Trip to Laguna Oviedo

Morning

🕐 Set off from **Barahona**, taking the coast road south. Drive slowly for the hairpin bends and to enjoy the views, with mountains on your right and the Caribbean Sea glistening to the left. Just as you enter **Paraiso** *(see p111)*, turn off to the left for a breathtaking lookout point. Then continue to **Los Patos**. Go over the humpback bridge over the River Patos, then turn left into the parking area where you will find the world's shortest river at just 200 feet long. Enjoy an early lunch of freshly caught fish with crispy plantain chips known as tostones, sat on the banks of the river.

Afternoon

After lunch continue on the same coast road all the way to **Oviedo**. Once you arrive at **Oviedo**, look out for the park office on the left, from where you can take a boat tour of **Laguna Oviedo**. There are a choice of tours that last for between 2 and 4 hours, and cost US$60–90 per boat. The laguna has more than 24 small islands, home to colonies of Rhinoceros Iguana, and is a birdwatcher's paradise, with heron, stern, golden spoonbill, frigate birds, pelicans, and red flamingos.

Retrace your journey back towards Barahona. Once you have passed Los Patos, turn right into **San Rafael** – another famous beach, where the river meets the sea. Bathe in the river's clear waters and sip a rum and coke from one of the beach shacks before heading back to Barahona.

At Parque Nacional de Isla Cabritos, it may be worth waiting to see if anyone else wants a boat trip in order to share the cost

Playa Cabo Rojo

Best of the Rest

1 Playa Najayo
A favorite beach with residents of Santo Domingo and San Cristóbal, this strip of golden sand isn't quiet, but it's a good place for a drink and a meal. ◎ Map E5

2 Playa Palenque
This beach is another popular hangout for locals, especially families. There is excellent food available at Cocolandia at the western end of the beach. ◎ Map D5

Bahía de las Aguilas

3 Playa Quemaito
One of the first beaches on the long and scenic road south of Barahona (see p110), this is a lovely and little-known stretch of wild coastline, backed by rugged cliffs and woods. ◎ Map B5

4 Larimar Mines
A rough track leads inland from the village of El Arroyo to the open-cast mines where semi-precious larimar is excavated. You can buy pieces of the blue mineral. ◎ Map B5

5 Baoruco
This charming fishing village, with the small Hotel Casa Bonita nearby in the hills, is situated close to a beach with white pebbles (see p45), behind which steep wooded hillsides tumble down towards the sea. ◎ Map B5

6 Paraíso
The small seaside town called Paradise is aptly named, with a gorgeous, if somewhat unkempt beach. It's shaded by sea grape trees (see p64) and bisected by a cool freshwater stream. ◎ Map B5

7 Polo Magnético
Up in the hills from Cabral is a scientific enigma – a stretch of road that appears to run upwards, but in fact descends. Take off your handbrake and see. ◎ Map B5

8 Cabo Rojo
A desolate expanse of gray sand and rocky bluffs, this empty empty beach (see p45) shows the scars of bauxite extraction. But it's a wildlife paradise for pelicans and other seabirds. ◎ Map A6

9 Bahía de las Aguilas
Few visitors make it to this deserted spot, a sweeping bay surrounded by rocky terrain. It's named after eagles, but there are more gulls, waders, and pelicans on display (see p45). ◎ Map A6

10 El Aguacate
As remote a place as you're likely to find, up a tortuous mountain road from Pedernales (see p111). The tiny border post of El Aguacate (Avocado) is almost lost among pine forests and clouds. ◎ Map A5

Around the Dominican Republic – The Southwest

A four-wheel-drive is essential to reach Larimar mines

Left & Right **Brisas del Caribe, Barahona**

TOP 10 Restaurants

1 Aubergine
Located in the hills southwest of Santo Domingo, Aubergine serves European dishes with an Asian twist. ◎ *Map D4 • Cambita Garabito, La Colonia, Km 6.5, San Cristóbal • 809 374 1382 • Open noon–11pm Fri & Sat, to 9pm Sun. Closed Mon–Thu • $$$$$*

2 Pizzeria d'Lina
Family-run restaurant serving pizza, plato del dia, meat, and seafood. Dine at a table on the quiet, pleasant patio and enjoy the excellent service. ◎ *Map B5 • Ave 30 Mayo, Barahona • 524 3681 • Open 7am–midnight daily • $$*

3 Cira
The tables at this friendly place with a family ambience, are set in the garden amid trees and flowers. The menu is based mostly around goat and fish. ◎ *Map C4 • Av Francisco del Rosario Sánchez 101, Azua • 809 521 3740 • Open 9:30am–10pm daily • $$*

4 Francia
Large helpings of good value, traditional Dominican dishes, served in simple surroundings. ◎ *Map C4 • Av Francisco del Rosario Sánchez 104, Azua • 809 521 2900 • Open 9am–10pm daily • $$*

5 Las Salinas
Casual bar and restaurant overlooking Las Salinas *(see p109)*. Popular with sailors for its seafood, burgers, and pasta. ◎ *Map D5 • Puerto Hermoso 7, Baní • 809 866 8141 • Open 7am–2am daily • $$$$*

6 Los Robles
The most popular restaurant in town, Los Robles serves good international and local cuisine at reasonable prices. ◎ *Map B5 • Av Enriquillo/Nuestra Señora de la Rosario, Barahona • 809 524 1629 • Open 9am–2am daily • $$*

7 La Casona
A popular choice with local workers, who head here for lunch, this restaurant has a pretty courtyard, boasts great service, and offers a wide variety of traditional Dominican dishes. ◎ *Map B5 • Calle Uruguay, Barahona • Open 10am–6pm • $*

8 Brisas del Caribe
The best restaurant in town, with delicious seafood and good service in pleasant surroundings. Packed at lunchtime. ◎ *Map B5 • Brisas del Caribe, Malecón, Barahona • 809 524 2794 • Open 9am–midnight • $$$*

9 Mesón Suiza
Dominican and international dishes are served with a Swiss touch, just a few blocks from Parque Central. ◎ *Map C4 • Calle 19 de Marzo 121, Azua • 809 521 9821 • Open 11am–11pm • $$*

10 Casa Bonita
Eat al fresco in a lovely setting on a hillside overlooking nearby Baoruco beach. The restaurant, open all day, is busy in Dominican holidays *(see p132)*.

Around the Dominican Republic – The Southwest

➤ Following pages **Women at an art stall, Sosúa Beach**

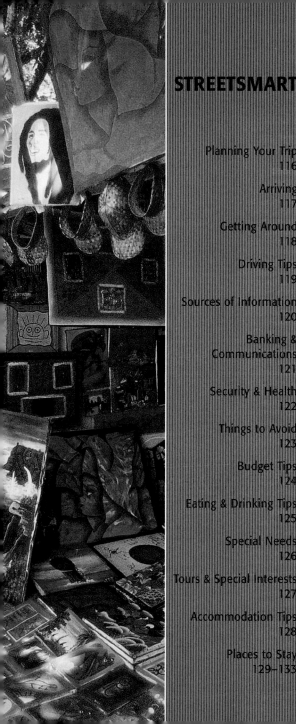

STREETSMART

DOMINICAN REPUBLIC'S TOP 10

Left **Cable car, Pico Isabel de Torres** Right **Sosúa Beach**

Planning Your Trip

1 Seasons

The country's main tourist season usually runs from December through April, when fares and accommodation are at their dearest. This period is rather drier and less warm than the rest of the year, but temperatures still average 77°F (25°C). The hurricane season lasts from June to November, with most storms occurring from August onwards, but the weather can still be fair.

2 Passports & Visas

All visitors must have a valid passport as well as a tourist card, which can be purchased at the airport on arrival. Visitors must also be in possession of an outward ticket. A departure tax of $20 is payable on leaving the country – this is usually included in the ticket price. It's worth photocopying passport details in case of theft or loss.

3 Currency

The Dominican currency is the peso (RD$), divided into 100 centavos. Dollars and euros are accepted in tourist areas, but you will get a better exchange rate if you change them to pesos before shopping.

4 Customs Regulations

Visitors are allowed to bring in 200 duty-free cigarettes and 2 liters of spirits. Customs searches tend to be relaxed, but the Dominican authorities take an extremely hard line on anything linked to firearms or illegal drugs. Food products, especially meat or dairy produce, are confiscated.

5 Insurance

Medical insurance is a must, as any illness or accident will involve paying for treatment and medication, and the best private facilities can be expensive. It is also worth having insurance cover against loss or theft of valuables. Visitors intending to carry out sporting activities such as scuba diving or whitewater rafting should ensure that they are covered.

6 Packing

Don't forget the essentials for a beach holiday, as swimwear can be expensive if bought locally. Visitors should also take a few formal jackets for dining out or nightlife, and it's certainly a good idea to have long trousers and long-sleeved shirts for mosquito-infested areas. Those intending to visit the "Dominican Alps" should remember that it can be chilly at night.

7 Health Precautions

There are no particular inoculation requirements for those entering the country, but travelers are advised to ensure that they are protected against tetanus, polio, and Hepatitis A and B. Malaria is a risk in the remote border areas near Haiti. There are occasional outbreaks of dengue and cholera, so follow the usual health precautions. Do not forget to bring prescription drugs.

8 Insect Repellent

This is one of the most vital things to bring with you. It should be applied liberally on exposed skin, especially ankles, and particularly at nightfall. Avoiding mosquito bites is an essential part of staying healthy in the Dominican Republic.

9 Electricity

The country's erratic electricity supply works on a 110-volt system, as in the US and Canada. Plugs are the two-pin North American type, so visitors from Europe may require suitable adaptors. While most Dominicans endure lengthy daily power cuts, due to a creaking power network, nearly all tourist facilities enjoy the benefits of private generators or inverters.

10 Independent Travel

Although some travelers would prefer to be independent and avoid all-inclusive packages, it is worth remembering that pre-booked package deals are almost always better value than last-minute arrangements.

Cruise ship, Santo Domingo

TOP 10 Arriving

1 International Airports

Your point of arrival is normally determined by where you are staying, whether in Santo Domingo or one of the principal tourist regions. These have their own international airports. Most scheduled flights land at Las Américas, near Santo Domingo.

2 Tourist Cards

Tourists must present a tourist card at passport control. The card costs US$10 and is valid for 30 days. Cards are available at all airports and must be filled in before going through immigration. They can also be bought online from your local Dominican Republic embassy website.

3 Changing Money at the Airport

It is unlikely that you will arrive already in possession of Dominican pesos, so the airport is a good place to exchange currency *(see p116)*. The Banco de Reservas offers a money-changing service at Las Américas, in Santiago, and Puerto Plata. There are also ATMs at all the airports, although these are sometimes empty during high season.

4 Touts

Incoming flights are often met by hordes of touts, offering services such as hire cars, money exchange, and guided tours. It is always sensible to decline their offers politely. Visitors arriving on pre-booked holiday packages are met by *bona fide* representatives.

5 From Las Américas into Santo Domingo

The Aeropuerto Internacional de las Américas is about 8 miles (13 km) east of the city center. There is no bus service, so it's best to take a taxi into town. Choose an official taxi driver (look for a brown certificate on the windscreen) and agree the price (about US$30) before setting off.

6 Punta Cana Airport

Most of the Punta Cana-Bávaro hotel complexes are within 30 minutes' drive of Punta Cana International airport, a rather picturesque cluster of thatch-roofed buildings. Hotels usually organize air-conditioned buses to pick up guests, however, taxis are always available, costing about US$40 to travel to most hotels.

7 Puerto Plata Airport

Situated between Puerto Plata and Sosúa, the Aeropuerto Internacional Gregorio Luperón is the main entrance point for North Coast visitors. A 15-minute drive into Puerto Plata, or any of the Playa Dorada hotels, costs around US$33.

8 Other Airports

There are also airports at Santiago (Cibao International), La Romana (used mostly for flights to Casa de Campo), Samaná (Presidente Juan Bosch), Barahona (María Montéz), and Santo Domingo (Dr Joaquín Balaguer).

9 Arriving by Boat

Several cruise lines include the Dominican Republic on their itineraries, stopping at the port in Santo Domingo, La Romana, or Samaná.

10 Ports of Entry

Official ports of entry for independent sailors are Santo Domingo, Puerto Plata, Luperón, Samaná, and Punta Cana. A customs fee of US$10 is applicable per person, payable at the customs and immigration facility, granting immigration clearance for 30 days.

Directory

International Airports
• Las Américas; 809 947 2220 • Punta Cana: 809 959 2376
• Gregorio Luperón: 809 291 0000
• Santiago: 809 233 8000 • Dr Joaquín Balaguer: 809 826 4019
• Samaná, Presidente Juan Bosch: 809 338 5888
• La Romana: 809 813 9000

See p127 for more information on tour operators

117

Left **Bus station, Santo Domingo** Right **Dominican Taxi**

10 Getting Around

1 Internal Flights
There are three domestic airlines: Fly Dominicana, Dominican Shuttles, and Caribbean Jet. Scheduled services operate between Samaná and Punta Cana, Punta Cana and Santo Domingo, plus Santo Domingo and Haiti. Private air charter transfers are available between all of the country's airports; they are much more expensive than the alternatives, but useful if you are in a hurry.

2 Long-Distance Buses
Very good value and surprisingly comfortable bus connections are provided by several companies and cover the entire country. Metro is good for North Coast destinations, while Caribe Tours has a comprehensive network of buses west and north of the capital. Nearly all buses are air-conditioned, with toilets and good seats. A great way to explore the Dominican Republic.

3 Taxis
There's no shortage of taxis, especially in tourist areas. Your hotel will be able to recommend a reputable local firm or call a taxi on your behalf, but always agree the price before setting off as all are unmetered. Many drivers are friendly and knowledgeable, and can be hired as a taxi-guide for an excursion.

4 Públicos & Guaguas
Públicos are private cars that act as shared taxis, plying fixed routes and normally crammed with passengers. *Guaguas*, on the other hand are mini-vans that start from a local bus station and are ideal for short trips without luggage.

5 Motoconchos
The ultimate low-budget option, the *moto-concho (see p123)* is a small motorbike, where the passenger sits on the pillion. Quite speedy but also dangerous.

6 Car Rental
Car rental is widely available but quite expensive, so do book ahead with one of the more established international companies such as Hertz or Avis. Local operators Nelly are good.

7 Motorcycles
You can easily hire a motorcycle at any of the main tourist areas, normally a small but still quite powerful Honda or Suzuki. Expect to pay US$25–30 per day.

8 Bicycles
Bicycles can be rented from specialist firms such as Iguana Mama *(see p127)* or from some of the beach resorts. Helmets should always be worn, and caution taken on main roads and in urban areas.

9 Ferries
There are two regular ferry services in the country. One links the port of Samaná with Sabana de la Mar across the Bay of Samaná. The other is a 12-hour overnight journey from Santo Domingo to Puerto Rico.

10 On Foot
Apart from hiking in the Cordillera Central, walking isn't much practised by visitors, though it's a practical way of exploring city centers such as Santo Domingo's Zona Colonial, the heart of Puerto Plata, or Santiago. Don't forget to bring comfortable shoes.

Directory

Internal Flights
• www.dominican shuttles.com • www. fly-dominicana.com
• www.caribbean jet.com

Buses
• Metro: 809 227 0101; www.metroservicios turisticos.com • Caribe Tours: 809 221 4422; www.caribetours. com.do

Car Rental
• Hertz: www.hertz.com
• Avis: www.avis.com

Ferries
• www.acferries.com
• www.horariode ferry.com

Left **Central La Romana** Right **A traffic light**

🔟 Driving Tips

Drive on the Right
If you're planning to rent a car, remember that driving can be challenging as well as exciting. In theory, Dominicans drive on the right, but overtaking vehicles often occupy the middle of the road, even on blind corners.

Animals
Animals, especially goats, present a threat in some of the Dominican Republic's more remote rural areas, as they tend to wander unchecked on to the road. This is a particular problem after nightfall when visibility is already limited. Dogs are also frequent victims of collisions.

After Dark
Driving after dusk is generally a risky business, as potholes, animals, and other obstacles are less clearly visible. Main thoroughfares are generally safer than isolated country roads, but bear in mind that some drivers have vehicles without working headlights and that others don't dip their headlights, causing dazzling among oncoming drivers. It's generally safer, except in well-lit urban streets, to stop driving before nightfall.

Speed Bumps
Most towns and villages have many speed bumps on their outskirts, often accompanied by a police or military check-point. These are meant to enforce the country's speed limits of 48 miles per hr (80 km/hr) on main roads and 25 miles per hr (40 km/hr) in towns.

Checkpoints
Particularly common in the regions closest to the Haitian border, these generally involve little more than slowing down and a nod or wave from a bored soldier. Occasionally, military personnel decide on a cursory inspection of a vehicle, but don't be alarmed.

Police
The Dominican police used to enjoy a certain notoriety for demanding bribes from motorists, often on the spurious pretext that a speed limit had been broken. This is much less common now, after a campaign by the authorities, but isolated cases do still occur. You can either hand the policeman a small note (US$1 or US$2) or simply insist that you do not speak Spanish until he gives up.

Tolls
The big *autopistas* out of Santo Domingo have automatic toll booths on exits from the capital. You will require US$1 per vehicle to go through. The *autopista* from Santo Domingo to Samaná will cost around US$10, split between three toll stations. The Atlantic Boulevard is US$12 each way and the Coral Highway also has tolls. All tolls must be paid in pesos.

Fuel
Gas is relatively expensive, due to rising world prices and a weak Dominican peso. Petrol stations (known as *bombas*) are plentiful in the main towns but sometimes extremely rare in remote country areas. It is worth filling up whenever possible. Many *bombas* close at about 8pm.

Flat Tires
Punctures are a constant problem on the country's poorly maintained road network and when driving on rough tracks. It can be extremely expensive to buy new tires, and a much cheaper option is to use the services of one of the legions of tire repair men (*gomeros*), whose workshops are to be found in every town.

Traffic Lights
Most Dominican towns are built on a classic grid system, with alternating up and down streets and traffic lights at intersections. With the chronic problem of power supply, however, traffic lights often don't work, so it is advisable to approach each junction on the assumption that any other car will fail to give way.

Left **News stand, Barahona** Right **White-water rafting, Jarabacoa**

Sources of Information

1 Tourist Offices Abroad

Official Dominican tourist offices in the United States, Canada, and the United Kingdom provide brochures and routine information on major destinations. For more details on specific activities, smaller hotels, and independent travel you may be better off consulting independent agencies, tourist offices, and websites.

2 Local Tourist Offices

There are tourist offices scattered throughout the country, with the main offices situated in Santo Domingo, but few have the resources or expertise to answer more than the most basic questions. A better bet would be one of the many specialist tour operators (see p127).

3 Websites

There is a huge amount of information about the country available on the Internet. Search engines are a useful means of locating specific information.

4 English-Language News

There is currently no English-language newspaper published in the Dominican Republic, but an invaluable source of news and general information is available on the website DR1, which has a daily news service as well as lots of material on travel and tourism.

5 Spanish-Language Press

There is a lively local press, with several daily and evening titles published in Santo Domingo. Some are available online, such as *Listín Diario*, *Diario Libre*, *Hoy*, and *El Caribe*.

6 Local Travel Agencies

Dotted around the country, these are often a reliable source of information on specific regions and activities.

7 Maps

There are several good maps of the country, the best published by Berndtson & Berndtson. In Santo Domingo, the best outlet for maps is Mapas Gaar (www. mapasgaar.com.do).

8 Bookstores

Several bookstores in Santo Domingo have a good range of maps, guidebooks, and other travel-related literature.

9 Guides

Although some individuals offering their services as guides can be a nuisance, there are many well-qualified and informed guides. Ask at your hotel or among any local contacts for a recommended and reliable person, who may also be a taxi driver (see p118).

10 Adventure Trips

For sports and activity holidays it is worth consulting Dominican Adventures' website *www.drpure.com* for maps, information, and a great many useful links.

Directory

Tourist Offices Abroad
• US: 1 (212) 588 1012
• Canada: 1 (514) 499 1918 • UK: 0207 242 7778

Local Tourist Offices
• Santo Domingo: Isabel la Católica 103, Plaza Colón • Puerto Plata: Calle José del Carmen Ariza 45 • Santiago: Ayuntamiento, Calle Duarte • Samaná: Av Santa Bárbara 4

Websites
• www.hispaniola.com
• www.colonialzone-dr. com • www.dr1.com

News Sources
• Listín Diario: www. listin.com.do • Diario Libre: www.diariolibre. com • Dominican Today: www.dominicantoday. com • El Caribe: www. elcaribe.com.do • Hoy: www.hoy.com.do

Map & Book Stores
• Mapas Gaar: El Conde & Espaillat 303, Santo Domingo
• Librería La Trinitaria, Arzobispo Nouel 160, Santo Domingo

Left **Public phones, Santo Domingo** Right **Internet café, North Coast**

TOP10 Banking & Communications

1 The Peso
The Dominican peso is divided into 100 centavos, with notes of 20, 50, 100, 200, 500, 1,000, and 2,000. The last two are often impossible to change, especially in rural areas. There are 1, 5, 10, and 25 peso coins in everday use. The peso's exchange rate against the US dollar and other currencies fluctuates widely, and there is an official rate announced daily in newspapers.

2 Using US Dollars
In tourist areas and all-inclusive hotels, prices are often quoted in US dollars, which are preferred to pesos. In more remote places, however, the peso is still the preferred currency.

3 Banks & ATMs
There are some foreign-owned and many local banks, all of which will change dollars at the official rate, though queuing at the counter can be a lengthy business. Opening hours are normally 8:30am–4pm, Monday to Friday. Major banks such as the Banco Popular, Banco León, and Banco de Reservas operate ATMs, which accept cards such as MasterCard and Visa.

4 Bureaux de Change
Casas de cambio offer more or less the same rates as banks and will cash traveler's checks. They also have longer opening hours than banks.

5 Credit Cards
The major cards are widely accepted in hotels, restaurants, and tourist-oriented stores, but not in out-of-the-way places or corner stores. Check the slip before signing and make sure that you are not charged in US dollars if you think you are paying in pesos. Credit cards can also be used for cash advances at certain banks, but this will involve at least 5 percent commission. There have been several incidents of the central credit card center copying cards, so try and use cash if possible.

6 Telephones
Public phones are plentiful and reliable, operated by several private companies. It's a good idea to buy a phone card (Claro) for between US$1 and US$6 *(see p124)*, which allows you to make cheap international calls. Avoid making calls from hotel rooms as these can be quite expensive.

7 Phone Codes
Calls made within the Dominican Republic require a 10-digit number which includes a 3-digit area code (809, 829, or 849). Long-distance calls and calls to cell phones require a prefix of 1. To call outside the country, dial 011 followed by the country code. To call the Dominican Republic from the United Kingdom dial 001, then the 10-digit number. From the US and Canada dial only the 1, then the 10-digit number (as for long distance calls within the country).

8 Charges
Phone charges can vary enormously, from exorbitant hotel rates to cheaper calls made from a phone center, where the operator dials for you and you sit in a booth. Calls between different towns and districts are charged at the same rate as those to the US. It is much cheaper in all cases to call before 8am, after midnight, or on Sundays.

9 Mail
Mail is slow, and you should not use street mail boxes. Special delivery (*entrega especial*) services are available at big post offices, but even these are unreliable. It is better to use an international courier company.

10 Internet
Internet services have expanded and improved dramatically but are still often victims of power cuts and technical problems. The main tourist areas now have a plethora of Internet cafés, and you are normally charged by the hour. Despite all the problems, email is still the best way of keeping in touch.

Phone cards can be easily purchased in shops on the streets of Santo Domingo – be sure to check the seal

Left **Police car, Santo Domingo** Center **Pharmacy, La Descubierta** Right **Bottled water**

Security & Health

Emergencies
The police and fire services can be contacted by dialing 911. Generally, the police are responsive to any reports of crime against tourists, although reporting a theft may involve a lengthy bureaucratic procedure. There are also special tourist police, known as Cestur, in all resort areas. Help is available from your relevant embassy or consulate. A private ambulance company, Movimed, in Santo Domingo, Santiago, and La Romana, can be reached on 809 532 0000.

Health Services
Public hospitals and clinics are rudimentary, however, there are excellent hospitals in Santiago and Santo Domingo. Your hotel will be able to recommend a doctor. In the event of a serious emergency, you should contact your insurance company.

Pharmacies
There are pharmacies in all the major towns, mostly well-stocked, and you do not necessarily require a prescription to obtain medicines. Check that the medicines you are given are not generic and cheaper versions, and that they are not past their sell-by date.

Personal Safety
Violent crime against foreigners is rare, but in tourist areas there is a risk of pick-pocketing and bag-snatching. Avoid dark and lonely spots, do not carry large amounts of cash, or flaunt expensive watches or phones, and keep valuables in the hotel, preferably in a safe.

Harassment
Most visitors experience some level of harassment, especially in well-trodden tourist areas, from individuals offering a range of services. Rudeness rarely produces a satisfactory outcome and may be counter-productive.

Police Stations
Every town and village has a police station, but few low-ranking officers will speak English. If you are the victim of theft, your hotel or embassy should be able to help you.

Consulates
The US, Canada, and UK all have embassies with consular services in Santo Domingo.

Women Travelers
Foreign women can receive a fair amount of unwanted attention from Dominican men, but this mostly takes the form of harmless verbal intrusions. The most effective response is a stony glare or cold indifference.

Food Hygiene
The best way to avoid an upset stomach is to steer clear of certain foods like meat, fish, and dairy products that have been allowed to stand too long on a buffet counter.

Water
Do not drink the tap water and make sure that ice cubes are made from purified water. Bottled water is cheap and widely available.

Directory

Medical Clinics
• Clínica Abreu: Beller 42, Santo Domingo, 809 688 4411 • UCE University Hospital: Av. Máximo Gómez, Santo Domingo, 809 221 0171 • Hospiten Bavaro: Higüey, 809 686 1414, www.hospiten.es • Hospiten Santo Domingo: 809 541 3000 • Hospital Metropolitan de Santiago (HOMS): 829 947 2222, www. homshospital.com • Centro Medico Bournigal: Puerto Plata, 809 586 2342, www. centromedicobournigal. com

Police Stations
• Calle Navarro, Santo Domingo, 809 682 2151 • Calle Genebra, Puerto Plata, 809 320 8840 • Av. Hispanoamerica, Santiago, 809 582 2331

Embassies & Consulates
• US: Santo Domingo, 809 221 2171 • Canada: Santo Domingo, 809 262 3100 • UK: Santo Domingo, 809 472 7111

Left **Dominican taxi** Right **Motoconchos, Las Terrenas**

TOP 10 Things to Avoid

1 Money-Changing Scams
Never accept the tempting offer of a better exchange rate from any would-be money-changer who approaches you. This informal money-changing system almost invariably involves a hefty rip-off, where you discover that you have a lot fewer pesos than were apparently counted out.

2 Taxi Scams
All taxis are unmetered, and although there are set prices for regular journeys, they are not widely visible. Most taxi drivers are honest, but a few will attempt to bamboozle visitors out of large sums. Always agree a price before setting off. Tourist taxis in front of hotels, airports, and bus stations charge twice the price of regular ones.

3 Traffic Jams
Roads in and around Santo Domingo can be appallingly congested, especially at rush hour (7–9am and 5–7pm) and at weekends and public holidays (see pp50–51), when a large number of the capital's inhabitants head for the beaches or mountains. Try to avoid traveling at peak periods, in particular Friday afternoons and evenings, and Sunday evenings. Congestion is particularly heavy when re-entering the capital Santo Domingo and attempting to cross the Ozama River into the city center.

4 Running Low on Gas
Fill up whenever possible, particularly if you are driving in the Cordillera Central or the remote northwest, as running out of fuel (see p119) can be time-consuming and highly expensive.

5 Running out of Cash
Banks (see p121) in the main towns are also often closed at weekends, although casas de cambio (bureaux de change) are more flexible in their opening times. When heading off into the country, make sure to withdraw enough cash to cover any eventuality.

6 Drugs
Though the Dominican Republic has less of a drugs culture than other Caribbean nations, there are still drug dealers in tourist resorts, offering cocaine, marijuana, and ecstasy at some night-clubs and other venues. The Dominican police take a very harsh view of all drug use and Dominican prisons are extremely unpleasant.

7 Sunstroke
It is easy, especially with children, to underestimate the power of the tropical sun, and sunburn and sunstroke are the most common threats to an enjoyable stay. Visitors should avoid the hottest part of the day, between noon and 3pm and cover themselves with a strong sunscreen, even when the weather seems predominantly cloudy. Drink plenty of water to avoid dehydration.

8 Mosquitoes
These annoying and potentially harmful insects are found in most parts of the country, especially near stagnant water and mangroves. Wear as much repellant (see p116) as possible and make sure that your room is fitted with a proper screen.

9 Sand Fleas
Although not particularly dangerous as such, the sand flea's bite is surprisingly painful. These creatures seem most active on beaches at dusk, but appear to be repelled by suntan lotion or baby oil. When bitten, hydrocortisone cream helps in reducing pain and itching.

10 Motoconchos
Motorbikes are the cheapest method of public transport (see p118). They are also physically dangerous not only for the unhelmeted passengers, but also for pedestrians, who are often involved in accidents with these vehicles. Look both ways before crossing the road.

Left **Shrimp and broccoli dish** Right **Tourists lounging at a bar, Playa Sosúa**

TOP 10 Budget Tips

1 Go Low-Season
You can save a good deal, both booking package deals and as an independent traveler, by visiting during the low season, between September and the middle of December. This is the end of the hurricane season, though this should not deter tourists.

2 Look for Budget Deals
Many travel agents offer substantial last-minute discounts, but this means that you will have to leave at short notice. It's also worth noting that prebooking all-inclusive deals is inevitably much cheaper than flying independently and then trying to book a room.

3 Look for Hotel Offers
If you are traveling independently, it is worth trying to negotiate cheaper rates at hotels, either by opting for a room-only arrangement or by haggling politely. Some Dominican hotels, especially in Santo Domingo and Santiago, will offer cheaper rates at weekends when commercial travelers are not using their rooms.

4 Public Transport
Buses and *guaguas* are a fraction of the price of hiring a car or taking a taxi and are a good way of seeing the countryside and meeting some local people. Though not luxurious, *guaguas* are regular and reliable and will get you from your hotel into town or to the beach for a few pesos.

5 Street Food
Cheap food on sale at street stands or in family-run *comedores* may present something of a health risk. But if you make sure that it is freshly cooked, a plate of chicken with rice and beans will cost little more than US$3. The principal rule is to have the food in question cooked in front of you and to avoid salads and fruit that may have been washed in tap water.

6 Happy Hours
Many hotels, bars, and restaurants operate an early evening happy hour, when drinks are half price or sometimes accompanied by complimentary snacks. The best time to look for two-for-one deals is between 6pm and 8pm, especially in the tourist areas.

7 Share a Guide
It can cut the cost of a guided tour or hiring a taxi driver/guide for a day by sharing with other visitors, as the guide will normally charge a fixed fee, irrespective of whether there is one or four clients. Taxis can also normally be shared between up to four people during trips.

8 Haggling
Most local stall-holders and shopkeepers not unreasonably assume that a tourist can afford to pay above the going rate for a T-shirt, necklace, or souvenir. Haggling is fine in places other than conventional supermarkets, and if you are persistent and polite, you may succeed in knocking down the price enough for you to feel you've got a bargain and the vendor to make a profit.

9 Avoid Tourist Stores
Shops and stores in tourist-oriented malls and hotels are often over-priced. You're much better off buying items such as soap or shampoo, liquor and snacks, from the local neighborhood *colmado*. Likewise, clothing and souvenirs are a good deal cheaper in open-air or covered markets, or in the informal beach markets in coastal resorts.

10 Buy a Phone Card
Making phone calls from hotel rooms can be very expensive. The best, and most economical, solution is to buy a phone card *(see p121)* which can be used with any phone, including the one in your room. Alternatively, if you have a triband cell phone, you can buy a local pre-paid SIM card for about US$7.

Left **Presidente Beer** Center **Brugal Rum Factory, Puerto Plata** Right **Hemingway's Café**

TOP 10 Eating & Drinking Tips

1 Restaurants, Cafeterías, & Comedores

Eating places in the Dominican Republic range from formal and swanky restaurants, where a meal can easily cost US$50 per head, to humble *cafeterías*, where the price is more likely to be under US$4. *Cafeterías* tend to offer a choice of precooked meals. On the other hand, *comedores*, or small local restaurants normally offer a single lunchtime dish.

2 Snacks & Fast Food

There are plenty of burger and chicken outlets in the main towns and tourist resorts, but more interesting are the Dominican versions of fast food available at snack stands. Cooked on demand and with high turnover, these tasty snacks are probably less risky than lukewarm buffet meals.

3 Breakfasts

Dominicans like a good filling breakfast, and most hotels will offer at least some local favorites such as *mangú*. There will always be a choice of tropical fruits, various breads and pastries and, of course, Dominican coffee.

4 Buffets

Buffets are the easiest way of feeding crowds of people at the same time in a large hotel. But they can be somewhat bland and boring, especially after a few days. The other problem is that food left standing around in the heat can easily attract a host of microbes, and many food poisoning cases have been traced to buffet food.

5 Fried Food

Dominican food, rather like its Spanish equivalent, is often heavy on the oil, with an emphasis on deep frying. Vegetables such as green beans have been known to arrive at table doused in oil. Some of the grease can be avoided by asking for grilled meat or fish known as *a la parrilla* or *a la plancha*.

6 Bills & Tipping

An 18 percent government tax is automatically added to restaurant bills, as is a 10 percent service charge. As it's very unlikely that your waiter or waitress will end up with that money, you should also leave a 10 percent tip, if you think the service merits it.

7 Beers & Wine

Wine is mostly imported from Spain or South America and is relatively expensive. The "house wine" at all-inclusives is often undrinkable. But Dominican beer, most conspicuously available under the Presidente label, is excellent and served ice cold in even the most remote village shop.

8 Rum

Rum is the serious drinker's first choice, and there are three very good brands: Brugal, Barceló, and Bermúdez, which come as dark or lighter varieties. *Añejo (see p55)* means aged, and is usually smoother and more expensive than the standard types. Avoid over-sugary cocktails and try a good rum like a brandy or on the rocks.

9 Bars

Outside tourist areas, where bars *(see pp58–9)* are often run by expats with a strong sense of how to please foreigners, Dominican bars can be rough-and-ready, dominated by machismo and not particularly comfortable for women. You're better off having a drink in the corner store, which usually has a well-stocked refrigerator. Bars tend to open and close late – as late as 2am on Friday and Saturday, and midnight Sunday through Thursday.

10 Buy a Bottle

On an evening out it's quite customary for groups to order a bottle of rum to share. It comes with a bucket of ice, and you can order soft drinks such as coke as a mixer.

 See also pp56–61 *for restaurants, bars and nightlife venues*

Left **Hotel Gran Almirante, Santiago** Center **Playa Sosúa** Right **A fruit punch**

Special Needs

1 Senior Travelers
All-inclusive hotels, in particular, have a long experience of meeting special needs in terms of mobility, and most are equipped with elevators and other amenities. In rural areas, however, there are fewer concessions to old age, and public lavatories or restrooms, for instance, are in very short supply.

2 Disabled Travelers
Some progress has been made in recent construction and refurbishment of hotel facilities, especially in the all-inclusive sector, to accommodate the needs of disabled travelers. But with the exception of a few well-trodden tourist sites, the country is not geared up for disabled needs, and there are no specially adapted cars.

3 Children
A few simple precautions such as not drinking tap water and excessive exposure to the sun should prevent avoidable health problems. There are plenty of activities for younger visitors (see pp36–37).

4 Childcare
Most of the big all-inclusives organize supervised children's activities on the beach or around the pool, usually in the form of a club. If you want to go out till late without children, it may

be possible to hire a baby-sitter. Ask at the hotel reception.

5 Diapers
Disposable diapers or nappies are available at the big supermarkets and drug stores, and sometimes, at a high price.

6 Prescription Medicines
Although most medicines are easily available at pharmacies and do not require a prescription, people with regular medicine requirements should bring more than what they estimate they will need in case of delay or emergency.

7 Vegetarians
Vegetarianism has yet to catch on in a big way, although there are vegetarian restaurant options in Santo Domingo and the tourist resorts. Non-meat eaters may be forced to make do with fried eggs or omelets as well as filling plantains and rice and beans. In the big hotels the choice is better, as buffets tend to feature a selection of salads and vegetable dishes.

8 Gay & Lesbian Travelers
The Dominican Republic is an overwhelmingly Catholic and macho society, and most people take an unsympathetic view of gay and lesbian relationships. Therefore, it's not a good idea for non-hetero-

sexual couples to go in for public displays of affection. Gay relations are not actually illegal, but harassment and even violence are not unknown. There is, on the other hand, an openly gay scene in the capital, and gay relationships are much more tolerated in the laid-back resorts of Sosúa, Las Terrenas, and Cabarete. A useful website for the local gay and lesbian scene is www.monaga.net.

9 Getting Married
Tying the knot in the Dominican Republic is a relatively straightforward affair, providing you have the appropriate documents, such as birth certificate, passport, and notarized certificate of single status. Although a Dominican wedding requires some forward planning, it is now an increasingly popular option. For more details, log onto www.santodom ingo.usembassy.gov or www.dominicanembassy. org.uk.

10 Getting Divorced
Only one married partner is required to be present at a Dominican "quickie" divorce, although divorce by mutual consent is much more straightforward than a contested divorce. The key to a smooth procedure is to find a reliable local lawyer. For advice, log onto www.international-divorce. com/d-dominican.html.

Left **Parque Nacional del Este** Right **Isla Catalina**

Tours & Special Interests

Tours of the Zona Colonial

Although the best way to explore Santo Domingo (see pp8–9) is on foot, there are several operators that offer tours. All tours will feature the services of an English-speaking guide. Another option is to take a ride in a horse-drawn carriage, which costs about US$20.

Tours of the Samaná Peninsula

The natural attractions of the Samaná Peninsula (see pp100–105) can be hard to reach if you don't know where you are going. Call on the services of a local operator such as Tour Samaná with Terry.

Tours of the North Coast

The beaches to the west of Puerto Plata are not easily accessible, and the trip to the historic site of La Isabela (see pp18–19) can be arduous. Operators based in and around Puerto Plata organize tours to a range of North Coast attractions as well as in the city of Puerto Plata (see pp94–9) itself.

Motorcycling Tours

Motorcycling tours offer a great way of seeing the country, from mountains to beaches, waterfalls, and lagoons. The tours are highly professional, run by MotoCaribe. The all-

inclusive package covers accommodation, meals, admissions, security, and guides.

Helicopter Tours

A short 20- or 30-minute helicopter flight over a spectacular stretch of coast or mountain landscape can be an unforgettable experience. Several companies, such as Helidosa, lay on flights for 2 or 3 passengers per trip.

Bird-Watching

The exciting range of the country's birdlife can be appreciated by amateurs or real connoisseurs, either by simply watching colorful birds in the hotel grounds or by seeking out rare species with a specialist operator such as Tody Tours.

Whale-Watching

The whale-watching season is between January and March and is concentrated around the Samaná Peninsula, where boats can take you out for short or longer expeditions. Whale Samana is one of several companies that organize tours that get you close to the playful whales.

Cycling

Cycling is probably the healthiest and most rewarding way to get off the beaten track and see real rural life. Iguana Mama and Caribbean

Bikes are experts in helping cyclists of all ages and abilities.

Diving

There are many diving companies around the island, either independent or attached to particular hotels. The Bayahibe area (see pp72–3) offers a good range of facilities for diving enthusiasts.

Fishing Trips

Small boats can be hired informally without too much difficulty at places such as Bayahibe or Palmar de Ocoa, but for big game fishing for marlin or bonito you'll need to contact a specialist operator such as Mike's Marina.

Directory

Local Tours
• www.cocotours.com
• www.dominican travel.com
• www.toursamana withterry.com

Activity Tours
• www.bavaro runners.com
• www.dive-centers. net
• www.todytours.com
• www.helidosa.com
• www.iguanamama. com
• www.mikes marina.info
• www.motocaribe.com
• www.whalesamana. com

Barceló Bávaro Beach Resort, Playa Bávaro

Accommodation Tips

1 Tipping
Tipping hotel staff is customary, but it's at your discretion. Porters usually expect a tip of around US$1 per bag carried to your room. If you leave US$1 a day in your room you'll find your house-keeper is more likely to put fresh flowers or elaborate towel decorations on your bed.

2 Location
Beachfront hotels will cost more than those off the beach and a room with a sea view will be costlier than one over-looking the garden. In Punta Cana nearly all the hotels are all-inclusive and you're not expected to stray far from your hotel. To explore the island, a North Coast destination is more convenient, with better public transport.

3 High Season
Prior booking is essential at Easter, when Dominicans take their holidays. In Cabarete there is a second high season, relating to windsurfing conditions, from June 15 to September 15.

4 All-Inclusives
Punta Cana, Bávaro, and Bayahibe in the East and Cofresí, Playa Dorada, and other North Coast beach resorts are dominated by all-inclusive hotels. Quality and service vary but basically you get what you pay for. Buffet food is monot-onous while alcoholic drinks are usually limited to national brands of rum and beer with watered down wine for dinner and extra charges for any-thing else. Check what's on offer, what sports you can opt for and for how long, whether there is an *à la carte* restaurant and how many times you can eat there. Some hotels require you to book your activities and meals days in advance, while others are more flexible.

5 Hotel Tax
All hotels charge an extra 28 percent on top of the room rate. This is made up of 18 percent sales tax and 10 percent service and is subject to change according to national taxation legis-lation. Room rates do not usually include the tax.

6 Accommodation Types
In Santo Domingo, hotels range from international style modern hotels run by foreign chains to boutique hotels in restored colonial man-sions. There are also a few cheap guesthouses and aparthotels. There are dozens of all-inclusive beach hotels on the North and East Coasts and several medium-sized ones for independ-ent travelers. Up in the mountains there are country inns and guesthouses offering comfortable lodging. Fewer options are available in the West.

7 Visitors with Disabilities
Very few hotels have facilities for the disabled. As there is no Dominican legislation requiring hotels to provide such amenities, it is best to try the international hotels where the parent company upholds the same standards world-wide *(see p126)*.

8 Air-Conditioning
Most medium and upper quality hotels have air-conditioning and their own generator as back up. Smaller hotels often suffer blackouts. Most places have ceiling or free-standing fans.

9 Language
Staff at hotels in the capital and resorts usu-ally speak English and often one other European language. In out of the way areas it is less common. A few Spanish phrases *(see p142)* will help you on excursions as well as in hotels.

10 Reservations
It is advisable to book at least your first few nights prior to arrival, although it is possible to travel around in low season without pre-booking. It is essential to book well in advance during the high season.

High season is December 15 to April 15, when hotel rates peak. For more information See p116

Ali's Surf Camp, Cabarete

TOP 10 Budget Hotels

1 Reina Ysabel, Santo Domingo

A friendly, family-run hotel, set above a music store in the heart of the shopping area of the old city. The rooms are basic but clean and adequate. Those with a balcony have a fan; some rooms have no windows though they have air-conditioning. Book in advance as it's usually full. ✆ Map N5 • El Conde 464 & Espaillat • 809 685 7692 • No smoking • $$

2 Hotel Discovery

Ideally situated opposite Independence Park, this 42-room hotel offers a great view of the Caribbean Sea from the fourth floor terrace, which also has a Jacuzzi. The hotel also has a restaurant and a cafeteria serving international cuisine. ✆ Map M6 • Arzobispo Nouel 402, Santo Domingo • 809 687 4048 • $$$ • www.discoverygranhotel.com

3 Aparthotel Roma

Located near el Conde, a popular shopping area in the Colonial Zone, this 60-room hotel is ideal for longer stays. All rooms are equipped with a safe, a flat screen TV, and Internet access. Some rooms also come with a kitchenette. ✆ Map N5 • Calle el Conde 206, corner of Av Duarte, Santo Domingo • 809 685 2022 • $$$ • www.aparthotelromard.com

4 Mi Casa, Constanza

In a central location, walking distance from transport, shops, and restaurants. There's also a *comedor* in the hotel that serves local food. ✆ Map C3 • Luperón y Sánchez • 809 539 2764 • $$

5 Brisas del Yaque, Jarabacoa

This place is excellent value for money. The rooms are small but the furnishings are in good condition. Rooms have a small balcony, a TV, and air-conditioning. There is no restaurant but the hotel is within walking distance of all the bars, cafés, and restaurants. ✆ Map C3 • Luperón esquina Peregrina Herrera • 809 574 4490 • $$

6 Colonial, Santiago

The rooms are small but well equipped with air-conditioning, good bathrooms with hot water, a fridge, and a TV. ✆ Map K2 • Av Salvador Cucurullo 115 • 809 247 3122 • $$

7 Ali's Surf Camp, Cabarete

Popular with surfers and kitesurfers, who are able to store their gear here. Equipment is also available to rent, and there is a regular shuttle service to El Encuentro and Kite Beach, the best surfing hotspots. Breakfast and dinner are included. ✆ Map D1 • Cabarete Procab, Calle Bahia 11 • 829 548 6655 • $$$ • www.alissurfcamp.com

8 Docia, Samaná

This guesthouse overlooks La Churcha with views of the bay and the dock below. The rooms are simple with private bathrooms and hot water. Each room has a fan. Those upstairs are brighter with large windows to catch the breeze. ✆ Map F2 • 809 538 2497 • $ • www.hotel docia.blogspot.com

9 Fata Morgana, Las Terrenas

Off the beaten track, this is a quiet, peaceful place popular with backpackers and budget travelers. The rooms sleep up to four people and have bathrooms. ✆ Map F2 • Turn off Fabio Abreu near the French school • 809 836 5541 • No air-conditioning • $ • www.fatamorganalas terrenas.com

10 Hotel Bayahibe, Bayahibe

The hotel lies within walking distance of dive shops and places to eat as well as the beach. Most rooms can sleep four and are equipped with two beds, a TV, fridge, air-conditioning, a balcony and en suite bathroom. There is Internet access in the lobby. ✆ Map G4 • Calle Principal • 809 833 0159 • $$$ • www.hotelbayahibe.net

Cabana Elke, Bayahibe

TOP 10 Self-Catering Hotels

1 Cayo Arena, Monte Cristi

A small complex of two-bedroom apartments on the seashore. The kitchens and bathrooms are basic but adequate. The complex has a small pool and a bar. ◊ Map A1 • Playa Juan de Bolaños • 809 579 3145 • $$$ • www.cayoarena.com

2 Anami Villas, Cabarete

A short drive west of Cabarete are these luxury furnished villas in the residential complex of Perla Marina. There's a shared pool and private beach. ◊ Map D1 • Cabarete Perla Marina • 809 571 0722 • $$$$$ • www.anamivillas.com

3 Palm Beach Condos, Cabarete

These roomy condos on the beach are privately owned, individually decorated, and are walking distance from the beaches and bars in Cabarete. ◊ Map D1 • 809 571 0758 • $$$$ • www.cabaretecondos.com

4 Bahía de Arena, Cabarete

A group of villas and apartments set on the outskirts of Cabarete, within walking distance of shops and restaurants. There is a communal area with a pool, Jacuzzi, tennis court, and small shop for essential supplies, as well as a Swiss restaurant. Guests must rent by the week.

◊ Map D1 • 809 571 0370 • $$$$–$$$$$ • www.cabaretevillas.com

5 Velero Beach Resort, Cabarete

One of the most luxurious hotels in Cabarete, offering flexible accommodation. Rooms and suites can be combined to make apartments, which have good kitchens and large living areas. All have a sea view. Good discounts in low season. ◊ Map D1 • Calle La Punta 1 • 809 571 9727 • $$$$ • www.velerobeach.com

6 Ocean Dream, Cabarete

Set on the beach, these apartments are ideal for families. There are two-, three-, and four-bedroom apartments, all equipped with balconies with a beach view. There's also a swimming pool and all kinds of activities from horseback riding and trekking to windsurfing and kiteboarding. ◊ Map D1 • 809 885 4080 • $$$ • www.oceandreamcabarete.com

7 Plaza Lusitana, Samaná

In the center of Las Galeras village, the suites and apartments are built above shops around a courtyard garden. Accommodation is spacious and has air-conditioning, fans, and tiled floors. Apartments have sofa beds in the living room. Suites are

large single rooms with a sitting area, kitchenette, and bathroom. ◊ Map F2 • Plaza Lusitana, Las Galeras • 809 538 0178 • $$$ • www.plazalusitana.com

8 Playa Colibrí, Las Terrenas

One of the larger complexes of studios and apartments with one or two bedrooms, a pool, Jacuzzi, and parking. You may negotiate daily, weekly, or monthly rates. ◊ Map F2 • Francisco Caamaño Deñó • 809 240 6434 • No air-conditioning • $$$ • www.hotelplayacolibri.com

9 Villa Baya Aparta-Hotel, Bayabibe

This small complex has eight apartments and nine rooms, all with kitchen, fridge, cable TV, and air-conditioning. There is also a restaurant serving seafood and pasta dishes. Accommodation is rented by the day, week, or month. ◊ Map G4 • Calle El Tamarindo • 809 833 0048 • $$ • www.villabayahotel.com

10 Cabana Elke, Bayahibe

Studio apartments in a small hotel just behind the all-inclusive Wyndham Dominicus Beach Resort (see p133), where you can buy a day pass to use the facilities. They also have a restaurant and a bar. ◊ Map G4 • Playa Dominicus • 809 860 4845 • $$$

Streetsmart

Most hotels now have websites and email addresses for booking on the Internet

Price Categories

For a standard, double room per night (with breakfast if included), taxes and extra charges.

$	under US$30
$$	US$30–US$50
$$$	US$50–US$100
$$$$	US$100–US$150
$$$$$	over US$160

Hostal Nicolás de Ovando, Santo Domingo

⏱10 Town Center Hotels

1 Hostal Nicolás de Ovando, Santo Domingo

This restored historic mansion dating from the 16th century features massive stone walls and high ceilings in every elegant room and suite. A pool overlooking the Río Ozama, a small state-of-the-art gym, and a gourmet restaurant complete the picture. ◈ Map P5 • Calle Las Damas • 809 685 9955 • Dis. access • $$$$$ • www.accorhotels.com

2 Hotel Francés, Santo Domingo

This small hotel set in a renovated colonial mansion with a central courtyard has a gourmet French restaurant. The rooms are elegant and comfortable. Buffet breakfast, tax, and service are included. ◈ Map P5 • Las Mercedes esq Arzobispo Meriño • 809 685 9331 • Dis. access • $$$$$ • www.accorhotels.com

3 Courtyard by Marriott, Santo Domingo

The rooms and service here are of an excellent standard and offer great value for money as breakfast is included. Free Internet access is available. They also have a gym, self-service laundry, a pool, restaurant, and delivery service from other restaurants. ◈ Map L3 • Av Máximo Gómez 50-A • 809 685 1010 • Dis. access • $$$$$

4 Sheraton Santo Domingo

An international Sheraton chain hotel offering rooms and suites for business and leisure travelers. It has a casino and good transport links. ◈ Map M4 • Av George Washington 365, Santo Domingo • 809 221 6666 • Dis. access • $$$$$ • www.starwoodhotels.com

5 Casa Sanchez, Santo Domingo

With a rooftop terrace, jacuzzi, and pool, this charming boutique hotel, situated in a beautifully restored colonial mansion in the center of the colonial zone, has it all. All rooms have air-conditioning, a safe, flat-screen TV, and Wi-Fi. ◈ Map N5 • Calle Sanchez 260, Zona Colonial • 829 947 9002 • Dis. access • $$$$ • www.casasanchez hotel.com

6 Hilton Hotel, Santo Domingo

Well-situated on the promenade, this award-winning skyscraper hotel boasts awe-inspiring views of the Caribbean through the floor-to-ceiling windows in every room. There is also a coffee maker in every room, plus Internet access, and guests can make use of the hotel's fitness center and pool. ◈ Map L4 • George Washington 500 • 809 685 0000 • Dis. access • $$$$$ • www3.hilton.com

7 Embassy Suites by Hilton, Santo Domingo

A brand new, all-suite hotel with a pool, fitness center, restaurant, and Wi-Fi. All rooms have air-conditioning, flat-screen TVs, and fully equipped kitchens. ◈ Map K2 • Ave Tiradentes and Gustavo Mejia Ricart • 809 685 0001 • $$$$$ • www.embassysuites3. hilton.com

8 El Beaterio, Santo Domingo

A guesthouse featuring a roof terrace and a patio. Airport transfers can be arranged. Breakfast included in the rates. ◈ Map N6 • Duarte 8 • 809 687 8657 • $$$$ • www.elbeaterio.com

9 Aloha Sol, Santiago de los Caballeros

Rooms are well appointed with air-conditioning, TV, good service, and the benefit of a restaurant on site. Breakfast included in the rates. ◈ Map C2 • Calle del Sol 150 • 809 583 0090 • Dis. access • $$$$

10 Hodelpa Gran Almirante Hotel & Casino, Santiago de los Caballeros

Popular with business travelers, the rooms here have a mini bar and Internet access. The hotel also has two restaurants and a pool. ◈ Map C2 • Av Estrella Sadhalá 10, Los Jardines • 809 580 1992 • Dis. access • $$$$$ • www.hodelpa.com

 For more information on Courtyard by Marriott or to make online bookings log onto www.marriott.com

Left **Rancho Baiguate, Jarabacoa** Right **Casa Bonita, Barahona**

TOP 10 Rural Hotels

1 Hotel Rancho Constanza & Cabañas de la Montaña, Constanza

Rancho Constanza has a modern Alpine-style block with rooms and basic cabins for families. There is a restaurant, a playground, and volleyball and basketball courts. The staff can arrange mountain sports. ✆ Map C3 • Colonia Kennedy, Frente a Politur • 809 682 2410 • No air-conditioning • $$ • www.rancho constanza.tripod.com

2 Alto Cerro

Accommodation ranges from camping to spacious self-catering villas, all spread along the hillside. The restaurant serves local meat, fruits, and vegetables. Horseback riding or quad-bike excursions can be arranged. ✆ Map C3 • East of Constanza heading to Colonia Kennedy • 809 530 6192 • No air-conditioning • $$$ • www.altocerro.com

3 Hotel Constanza, Constanza

This is a complex of small townhouses with kitchenettes, each of which can sleep four guests. Breakfast is provided but there is no restaurant. They also have a pool, a bar, and a volleyball court. ✆ Map C3 • Carretera Gen Antonio Duvergé, Colonia Japonesa • 809 539 2930 • No air-conditioning • $$$ • www.hotelconstanza.net

4 Rancho Baiguate, Jarabacoa

This place is known for adventure sports such as river rafting, tubing, hiking, and horse riding. The rooms vary in size, standard, and price, with meals included, but no TV, air-conditioning, or other modern conveniences. ✆ Map C3 • La Joya • 809 574 6890 • No air-conditioning • $$$$ • www.ranchobaiguate.com

5 Pinar Dorado, Jarabacoa

A single block of hotel rooms set in a pleasant garden surrounded by pine trees with a pool. It's comfortable but not remarkable. Air-conditioning and TV in all rooms, buffet breakfast, lunch, and dinner on offer. Meal plans are available. ✆ Map C3 • Carretera a Constanza 1km • 809 574 2820 • $$ • www.hotelpinardorado.com

6 Gran Jimenoa, Jarabacoa

Outside town on the edge of the Río Jimenoa, the rooms here are nothing fancy, but they are comfortable and come with a TV. Rates include breakfast and taxes. ✆ Map C3 • Av la Confluencia, Los Corralitos • 809 574 6304 • $$$ • www.granjimenoahotel.com

7 California, Jarabacoa

This small, family-run hotel has simple rooms with fans, all on the ground floor, leading out to a central patio and pool. Breakfast is US$9, while other meals of comida criolla can be arranged on request. Local activities can be arranged. ✆ Map C3 • Calle José Durán E 99 • 809 574 6255 • No air-conditioning • $ • www.hotelcaliforniajarabacoa.com

8 Blue Moon, Cabarete

Accommodation is in one of four individually decorated suites, a family suite, or a two-bedroom apartment with kitchen. Breakfast is included and the restaurant serves Indian food. ✆ Map D1 • Los Brazos • 809 757 0614 • $$$ • www.bluemoonretreat.net

9 Casa Bonita, Barahona

The rooms in these bungalows come with fans and air-conditioning but no TV or phone. The restaurant is good but rather expensive (see p113). ✆ Map B5 • Carretera de la Costa km 17 • 809 476 5059 • $$$$$ • www.casabonitadr.com

10 Aquarius, Bonao

The rooms and suites offer the latest communications technology and are designed for business travelers as well as vacationers. There is a restaurant, a mini bar, and a cocktail lounge. ✆ Map H4 • Calle Duarte 104 • 809 296 0303 • Dis. access • $$$ • www.aquariusbonao.com

Hotel staff at Aquarius can arrange excursions with boat rides to the Hatillo dam, caves, and rivers as well as horseback riding

Price Categories

For a standard, double room per night (with breakfast if included), taxes and extra charges.

$	under US$30
$$	US$30–US$50
$$$	US$50–US$100
$$$$	US$100–US$150
$$$$$	over US$150

Atlantis, Las Terrenas

ⁱ⁰ Beach Hotels

1 Sosúa-by-the-Sea

This pleasant hotel offers the advantages of booking either room-only or all-inclusive. The rooms are clean and tidy, with air-conditioning, and there is a pool. Northern Coast Diving is on site for scuba diving lessons and excursions. ◎ Map D1 • Sosúa • 809 571 3222 • $$$$ • www.sosuabythesea.com

2 Kitebeach, Cabarete

A kiteboarder's paradise, with accommodation packages including kite lessons, storage, repairs, and cleaning of all gear. You can choose budget or superior rooms, air-conditioned suites, or apartments. Negotiate special rates for long stays. Buffet breakfast is included and Internet access is free. ◎ Map D1 • 809 571 0878 • $$$ • www.kitebeachhotel.com

3 Villa Taína, Cabarete

Sit on the beachside restaurant and watch the windsurfers from the school next door. A short stroll along the sand takes you to various places to eat and drink, and to the nightlife venues of Cabarete. The rooms have air-conditioning, and a balcony or terrace. Breakfast is included in the rates. ◎ Map D1 • Calle Principal • 809 571 0722 • $$$ • www.villa taina.com

4 Playa Esmeralda Beach Resort, Guayacanes

Situated on a stunning sandy beach in the fishing village of Guayacanes, this 45-room hotel features lush tropical gardens, free Wi-Fi, and a fitness room. The rooms are basic but comfortable with a mini bar, air-conditioning, a safe, cable TV, and balcony. ◎ Map F4 • Paseo Vicini • 809 526 3434 • $$$ • www.playaesmeraldaresort.com

5 Bahía Blanca, Río San Juan

This is a wonderful place to admire the turquoise hues of the sea, so clear you can see the coral. The rooms are simple and clean with basic amenities. Meal plans are available. ◎ Map E1 • Gastón F Deligne 5 • 809 589 2528 • $$

6 Villa Serena, Las Galeras

The rooms are impeccably decorated and furnished with ceiling fans and air-conditioning, while the restaurant offers gourmet cuisine (see p104). ◎ Map F2 • 809 538 0000 • $$$$ • www.villaserana.com

7 Atlantis, Las Terrenas

This hotel is known for its French food. The rooms are large and comfortable with marble bathrooms. Some have air-conditioning. ◎ Map F2 • Playa Bonita • 809 240 6111 • $$$$ • www.hotel-atlantis-lasterrenas.com

8 Barceló Bávaro Beach Resort

An all-inclusive resort comprising five hotels, offering a golf course, a 24-hour casino, Internet café, shops, and a convention center. A small tram shuttles guests around the property. ◎ Map H4 • Playa Bávaro • 809 686 5797 • Dis. access • $$$$$ • www.barcelobavarobeach resort.com

9 Viva Wyndham Dominicus Palace/ Beach, Bayahibe

Two all-inclusive hotels for the price of one. The Palace is better and more expensive, but shares the Beach's private beach. There are many restaurants, but you have to reserve one day in advance for the à la carte ones. Also on offer: bars, disco, a theater, kids' club, soccer, and organized trips. ◎ Map G4 • Playa Dominicus • 809 686 5658 • Dis. access • $$$$$ • www.vivaresorts.com

10 Gran Bahía, Samaná

An all-inclusive, elegant hotel not normally found in Dominican resorts. The service is good and there are many facilities, including a 9-hole golf course and horse riding. Boat trips and whale-watching trips arranged. ◎ Map F2 • Carretera a Las Galeras • 809 538 2066 • Dis. access • $$$$ • www.bahia-principe.com

 Contact Northern Coast Diving (809 571 1028 or www.northern coastdiving.com) for information on excursions and scuba diving

General Index

Acknowledgments

The Author
James Ferguson is a writer and publisher who has specialized in the Caribbean for 20 years. He has written books on Haiti, the Dominican Republic, and Grenada and is a regular contributor to *Caribbean Beat* magazine.

Photographer Jon Spaull

Additional Photography
Deni Bown, Demetrio Carrasco, Andy Crawford, Eric Crichton, Hans-Ulrich Dillmann, Ken Findlay, Philip Gatward, Derek Hall, Colin Keates, Richard Leeney, David Murray, Rob Reichenfeld, Tim Ridley, Lucio Rossi, Jules Selmes, Clive Streeter, Debi Treloar, Jerry Young.

Cartography Credits Base mapping for Dominican Republic and Santo Domingo derived from Netmaps www.netmaps.es

AT DK INDIA:
Managing Editor Aruna Ghose
Art Editor Benu Joshi
Project Editor Vandana Bhagra
Editorial Assistance Pamposh Raina
Project Designers Baishakhee Sengupta, Divya Saxena
Senior Cartographer Uma Bhattacharya
Cartographer Alok Pathak
Picture Researcher Taiyaba Khatoon
Fact Checker Griselda Gonzalez Nin
Indexer & Proofreader Bhavna Seth Ranjan
DTP Co-ordinator Shailesh Sharma
DTP Designer Vinod Harish
AT DK LONDON:
Publisher Douglas Amrine
Publishing Manager Vicki Ingle
Managing Art Editor Jane Ewart

Senior Cartographic Editor Casper Morris
Senior DTP Designer Jason Little
DK Picture Library Romaine Werblow, Hayley Smith, Gemma Woodward
Production Shane Higgins
Revisions Team Namrata Adhwaryu, Ashwin Raju Adimari, Christopher Baker, Juliane Balke, Sonal Bhatt, Imogen Corke, Neha Dhingra, Hans-Ulrich Dillmann, Vidushi Duggal, Lindsay de Feliz, Emer FitzGerald, Niki Foreman, Anna Freiberger, Rhiannon Furbear, Camilla Gersh, Sumita Khatwani, Leena Lane, Hayley Maher, Catherine Palmi, Marianne Petrou, Lucy Richards, Ellen Root, Sands Publishing Solutions, Beverley Smart, Susana Smith, Leah Tether, Conrad van Dyk, Ajay Verma, Deepika Verma, Ros Walford, Dora Whitaker, Sophie Wright

Picture Credits
a-above; b-below/bottom; c-center; l-left; r-right; t-top.

The publisher would also like to thank the following for their assistance and kind permission to photograph at their establishments:

Acuario Nacional; Adrian Tropical; Aguaceros; Atlantis; Baoruco Beach Resort; Barceló Bávaro Beach Resort; Brisas del Caribe; Brugal Rum Factory; Cabana Elke; Café Cito; Casa Bonita; Casa de Campo; Columbus Aquapark; Crazy Moon; Hemingway's Café; Hodelpa Gran Almirante Hotel & Casino; Jet Set; José Oshay's Irish Beach Pub; La Casa del Pescador; La Isabela; La Résidence; Las Brisas; Las Salinas; Le Café de Paris; Librería Thesaurus; Mesón de la Cava;

Museo de Arte; Museo de Larimar; Museo del Hombre Dominicano; Museo Prehispánico; Museum at the Parque Nacional Histórico La Isabela; On the Waterfront; Paradise Resort; Rancho Baiguate; Sam's Bar & Grill; Sofitel Nicolás de Ovando; Tropical Lodge; Vesuvio; Wilson's Beach House.

The publishers would like to thank the following individuals, companies and picture libraries for their kind permission to reproduce their photographs.

ALAMY IMAGES: Age Fotostock 118tr, 123tl; Michael Dwyer 120 tl; Hemis 32tr; Reimar-5 78–9; ALI'S SURF CAMP, CABARETE: 129tl; RICHARD AMMON (GLOBAL GAYZ): 75tr.

THE BEACH RESTAURANT: 104tr.

CASA DE CAMPO: 24cla, 25tl, 25tr, 25cr, 25cb. CASA DE TEATRO 58tl. CASA VIENTIUNO: 90tl. CORBIS: 31tr; Tony Arruza 7bl, 8-9c; 21cr, 24-25c, 27cra; Tom Bean 37tr, 16-17c, 50c, 50tr,100t; Bettmann 30 tr, 31tl; Richard Bickel 12-13c; 110tc, 106-107, Duomo 39tr; Reinhard Eisele 68-69; Macduff Everton 23tl, 38bl; Franz-Marc Frel 6cl, 14-15c, 20-21c; Jeremy Horner 11cr; Patrick Johns 65bl; Danny Lehman 7cl, 22br 51bl, 114-115; Massimo Listri 28-29; Ludovic Maisant 49tr, 53tr; Douglas Peebles 64tl; Giraud Philippe 38tr; Carl & Ann Purcell 92-93; Joel W. Rogers 2tl, 4-5; Kevin Schafer 64c, 64tl; Jim Sugar 18clb; Nevada Wier 111bl. CLARA GONZALEZ www.DominicanCooking.com: 63bl.

DREAMSTIME.COM: William Berry 110bl.

GRAN BAHIA PRINCIPE EL PORTILLO: 21tr.

MONKEY JUNGLE: 36tc. MUSEO DE ARTE MODERNO DE LA REPÚBLICA DOMINICANA: 34tl.

PAT'E PALO EUROPEAN BRASSERIE: 57bl. PLATINUM: 60tr.

ROCKY'S ROCK AND BLUES BAR: 90tr.

VILLA SERENA: 104tl.

All other images © Dorling Kindersley

For further information see www.dkimages.com

Special Editions of DK Travel Guides

DK Travel Guides can be purchased in bulk quantities at discounted prices for use in promotions or as premiums. We are also able to offer special editions and personalized jackets, corporate imprints, and excerpts from all of our books, tailored specifically to meet your own needs.

To find out more, please contact:

(in the US) **SpecialSales@dk.com**

(in the UK) **TravelSpecialSales@uk.dk.com**

(in Canada) DK Special Sales at **general@tourmaline.ca**

(in Australia) **business.development@ pearson.com.au**

Phrase Book

Phrase Book

In an Emergency

Help!	¡Socorro!	soh-**koh**-roh
Stop!	¡Pare!	**pah**-reh
Call a doctor!	¡Llame a un médico!	**yah**-meh ah **oon** meh-**dee**-koh
Call an ambulance!	¡Llame una ambulancia!	**yah**-meh ah **oonah** ahm-boo-**lahn**-see-ah
Call the fire department!	¡Llame a los bomberos!	**yah**-meh ah lohs bohm-beh-rohs
policeman	el policía	ehl poh-lee-**see**-ah

Communication Essentials

English	Spanish	Pronunciation
Yes	Sí	see
No	No	noh
Please	Por favor	pohr fah-**vohr**
Thank you	Gracias	**grah**-see-ahs
Excuse me	Perdone	pehr-**doh**-neh
Hello	Hola	**oh**-lah
Bye (casual)	Chau	chau
Goodbye	Adiós	ah-dee-**ohs**
What?	¿Qué?	keh
When?	¿Cuándo?	**kwahn**-doh
Why?	¿Por qué?	pohr-**keh**
Where?	¿Dónde?	**dohn**-deh
How are you?	¿Cómo está usted?	**koh**-moh ehs-**tah** oos-**tehd**
Very well, thank you	Muy bien, gracias	mwee bee-**ehn grah**-see-ahs
Pleased to meet you	Mucho gusto	**moo**-choh **goo**-stoh
See you soon	Hasta pronto	ahs-tah **prohn**-toh
I'm sorry	Lo siento	loh see-**ehn**-toh

Useful Phrases

That's fine	Está bien	ehs-**tah** bee-**ehn**
Great/fantastic!	¡Qué bien!	keh bee-**ehn**
Where is/are...?	¿Dónde está/están...?	**dohn**-deh ehs-**tah**/ehs-**tahn**
How far is it to...?	¿Cuántos metros/ kilómetros hay de aquí a...?	**kwahn**-tohs **meh**-trohs/kee-**loh**-meh-trohs eye deh ah-**kee** ah
Which way is it to...?	¿Por dónde se va a...?	pohr **dohn**-deh seh **vah** ah
Do you speak English?	¿Habla inglés?	**ah**-blah een-**glehs**
I don't understand	No comprendo	noh kohm-**prehn**-doh
I would like	Quisiera/ Me gustaría	kee-see-**yehr**-ah meh goo-stah-**ree** ah

Useful Words

big	grande	**grahn**-deh
small	pequeño/a	peh-**keh**-nyoh/nyah
hot	caliente	kah-lee-**ehn**-teh
cold	frío/a	**free**-oh/ah
good	bueno/a	**bweh**-noh/nah
bad	malo/a	**mah**-loh/lah
open	abierto/a	ah-bee-**ehr**-toh/tah
closed	cerrado/a	sehr-**rah**-doh/dah
full	lleno/a	**yeh**-noh/nah
empty	vacío/a	**vah**-see-oh/ah
left	izquierda	ees-key-**ehr**-dah
right	derecha	deh-**reh**-chah
(keep) straight ahead	(siga) derecho	(**see**-gah) deh-**reh**-choh
near	cerca	**sehr**-kah
far	lejos	**leh**-hohs
more	más	mahs
less	menos	**meh**-nohs
entrance	entrada	ehn-**trah**-dah
exit	salida	sah-**lee**-dah
elevator	el ascensor	ehl ah-sehn-**sohr**
restrooms	baños/ servicios	**bah**-nyohs/
women's	de damas	deh **dah**-mahs
men's	de caballeros	deh kah-bah-**yeh**-rohs

Post Offices & Banks

Where can I change money?	¿Dónde puedo cambiar dinero?	dohn-deh **pweh**-doh kahm-bee-**ahr** dee-**neh**-roh
How much is the postage to...?	¿Cuánto cuesta enviar una carta a...?	**kwahn**-toh **kweh**-stah ehn-vee-**yahr oo**-nah **kahr**-tah ah
I need stamps	Necesito estampillas	neh-seh-**see**-toh ehs-tahm-**pee**-yahs

Shopping

How much does this cost?	¿Cuánto cuesta esto?	**kwahn**-toh **kwehs**-tah **ehs**-toh
I would like...	Me gustaría...	meh goos-tah-**ree**-ah
Do you have?	¿Tienen?	tee-**yeh**-nehn
Do you take credit cards?	¿Aceptan tarjetas de crédito/	ahk-**sep**-tahn tahr-**heh**-tahs deh **kreh**-dee-toh/
traveler's checks?	cheques de viajero?	**cheh**-kehs deh vee-ah-**heh**-roh
I am looking for...	Estoy buscando...	ehs-**toy** boos-**kahn**-doh
expensive	caro	**kahr**-oh
cheap	barato	bah-**rah**-toh
white	blanco	**blahn**-koh
black	negro	**neh**-groh
red	rojo	**roh**-hoh
yellow	amarillo	ah-mah-**ree**-yoh
green	verde	**vehr**-deh
blue	azul	ah-**sool**

142

antiques store	la tienda de antigüedades	lah tee-**ehn**-dah deh ahn-tee-gweh-**dah**-dehs
bakery	la panadería	lah pah-nah-deh-**ree**-ah
bank	el banco	ehl **bahn**-koh
bookstore	la librería	lah lee-breh-**ree**-ah
butcher's	la carnicería	lah kahr-nee-seh-**ree**-ah
cake store	la pastelería	lah pahs-teh-leh-**ree**-ah
jeweler's	la joyería	lah hoh-yeh-**ree**-yah
market	el mercado	ehl mehr-**kah**-doh
newsstand	el kiosko de prensa	ehl kee-**ohs**-koh deh **prehn**-sah
post office	la oficina de correos	lah oh-fee-**see**-nah deh kohr-**reh**-ohs
shoe store	la zapatería	lah sah-pah-teh-**ree**-ah
supermarket	el supermercado	ehl soo-pehr-mehr-**kah**-doh
travel agency	la agencia de viajes	lah ah-**hehn**-see-ah deh vee-**ah**-hehs

Transportation

When does the... leave?	¿A qué hora sale el...?	ah **keh oh**-rah **sah**-leh ehl
Where is bus stop?	¿Dónde está la parada de buses?	**dohn**-deh ehs-the **tah** lah pah-**rah**-dah deh **boo**-sehs
Is there a bus to...?	¿Hay un autobús/ guagua...a?	**eye oon** ow-toh-**boos**/**gwah**-gwah ah
ticket office	la taquilla	lah tah-**kee**-yah
round-trip ticket	un boleto de ida y vuelta	**oon** boh-**leh**-toh deh **ee**-dah ee voo-**ehl**-tah
one-way ticket	un boleto de ida solamente	**oon** boh-**leh**-toh deh **ee**-dah soh-lah-**mehn**-teh
airport	el aeropuerto	ehl ah-ehr-oh-poo-

Sightseeing

art gallery	el museo de arte	ehl moo-**seh**-oh deh **ahr**-teh
beach	la playa	lah **plah**-yah
cathedral	la catedral	lah kah-teh-**drahl**
church	la iglesia/	lah ee-**gleh**-see-ah/
garden	el jardín	ehl hahr-**deen**
museum	el museo	ehl moo-**seh**-oh
ruins	las ruinas	lahs roo-**ee**-nahs
tourist information office	la oficina de turismo	lah oh-fee-**see**-nah deh too-**rees**-moh
ticket	la entrada	lah ehn-**trah**-dah

guide (person)	el/la guía	ehl/lah **gee**-ah
guide (book)	la guía	lah **gee**-ah
map	el mapa	ehl **mah**-pah
taxi stand	sitio de taxis	**see**-tee-on deh **tahk**-sees

Staying in a Hotel

Do you have a vacant room?	¿Tienen una habitación libre?	tee-**eh**-nehn **oo**-nah ah-bee-tah-see-**ohn lee**-breh
double room	habitación doble	ah-bee-tah-see-**ohn doh**-bleh
single room	habitación sencilla	ah-bee-tah-see-**ohn** sehn-**see**-yah
room with a bath	habitación con baño	ah-bee-tah-see-**ohn** kohn **bah**-nyoh
shower	la ducha	lah **doo**-chah
I have a reservation	Tengo una habitación reservada	tehn-goh **oo**-nah ah-bee-tah-see-**ohn** reh-sehr-**vah**-dah
key	la llave	lah **yah**-veh

Eating Out

Have you got a table for...	¿Tienen una mesa para...?	tee-**eh**-nehn **oo**-nah meh-sah pah-**rah**
I want to reserve a table	Quiero reservar una mesa	kee-eh-roh reh-sehr-**vahr oo**-nah meh-sah
The bill, please	La cuenta, por favor	lah **kwehn**-tah pohr fah-**vohr**
I am a vegetarian	Soy vegetariano/a	soy veh-heh-tah-ree-**ah**-no/na
waiter/waitress	camarero/a	kah-mah-**reh**-roh/rah
menu	el menú	ehl meh-**noo**
wine list	la carta de vinos	lah **kahr**-tah deh **vee**-nohs
glass	un vaso	**oon vah**-soh
bottle	una botella	**oo**-nah boh-**teh**-yah
knife	un cuchillo	**oon** koo-**chee**-yoh
fork	un tenedor	**oon** teh-neh-**dohr**
spoon	una cuchara	**oo**-nah koo-**chah**-rah
breakfast	el desayuno	ehl deh-sah-**yoo**-noh
lunch	la comida	lah koh-**mee**-dah
dinner	la cena	lah **seh**-nah
main course	el plato fuerte	ehl **plah**-toh foo-**ehr**-teh
starters	las entradas	lahs ehn-**trah**-das
dish of the day	el plato del día	ehl **plah**-toh dehl **dee**-ah
tip	la propina	lah proh-**pee**-nah
Is service included?	¿El servicio está incluido?	ehl sehr-**vee**-see-oh ehs-**tah** een-kloo-**ee**-doh

Bold letters in the pronunciation guides (third columns) indicate the stressed syllable

Menu Decoder

el aceite	ah-**see-eh**-teh	oil
las aceitunas	ah-**seh-toon**-ahs	olives
el agua mineral	**ah**-gwa mee-neh-**rahl**	mineral water
sin gas/con gas	seen gas/kohn gas	still/sparkling
el ajo	**ah**-hoh	garlic
el arroz	ahr-**rohs**	rice
el azúcar	ah-**soo**-kahr	sugar
una bebida	beh-**bee**-dah	drink
el café	kah-**feh**	coffee
la carne	**kahr**-neh	meat
la cebolla	seh-**boh**-yah	onion
la cerveza	sehr-**veh**-sah	beer
el cerdo	**sehr**-doh	pork
el chocolate	choh-koh-**lah**-teh	chocolate
la ensalada	ehn-sah-**lah**-dah	salad
la fruta	**froo**-tah	fruit
el guineo	gee-**nee**-ee-oh	banana
el helado	eh-**lah**-doh	ice cream
el huevo	oo-**eh**-voh	egg
el jugo	ehl **hoo**-goh	juice
la langosta	lahn-**gohs**-tah	crayfish
la leche	**leh**-cheh	milk
la mantequilla	mahn-teh-**kee**-yah	butter
la manzana	mahn-**sah**-nah	apple
los mariscos	mah-**rees**-kohs	seafood
la naranja	nah-**rahn**-hah	orange
el pan	**pahn**	bread
las papas	**pah**-pahs	potatoes
el pescado	pehs-**kah**-doh	fish
picante	pee-**kahn**-teh	spicy
la pimienta	pee-mee-**yehn**-tah	pepper
el pollo	**poh**-yoh	chicken
el postre	**pohs**-treh	dessert
el queso	**keh**-soh	cheese
el refresco	reh-**frehs**-koh	soft drink/soda
la sal	**sahl**	salt
la salsa	**sahl**-sah	sauce
la sopa	**soh**-pah	soup
el té	**teh**	herb tea
el té negro	teh **neh**-groh	tea
la torta	**tohr**-tah	sandwich
las tostones	tohs-**to**-nes	fried plantains
el vinagre	vee-**nah**-greh	vinegar
el vino blanco	**vee**-noh **blahn**-koh	white wine
el vino tinto	**vee**-noh **teen**-toh	red wine

Numbers

	Spanish	Pronunciation
0	cero	**seh**-roh
1	uno	**oo**-noh
2	dos	dohs
3	tres	trehs
4	cuatro	**kwa**-troh
5	cinco	**seen**-koh
6	seis	says
7	siete	**see**-eh-teh
8	ocho	**oh**-choh
9	nueve	**nweh**-veh
10	diez	dee-**ehs**
11	once	**ohn**-seh
12	doce	**doh**-seh
13	trece	**treh**-seh
14	catorce	kah-**tohr**-seh
15	quince	**keen**-seh
16	dieciséis	dee-eh-see-**seh-ees**
17	diecisiete	dee-eh-see-see-**eh**-teh
18	dieciocho	dee-eh-see-**oh**-choh
19	diecinueve	dee-eh-see-**nweh**-veh
20	veinte	**veh**-een-teh
21	veintiuno	veh-een-tee-**oo**-noh
22	veintidós	veh-een-tee-**dohs**
30	treinta	**treh**-een-tah
31	treinta y uno	treh-een-tah ee **oo**-noh
40	cuarenta	kwah-**rehn**-tah
50	cincuenta	seen-**kwehn**-tah
60	sesenta	seh-**sehn**-tah
70	setenta	seh-**tehn**-tah
80	ochenta	oh-**chehn**-tah
90	noventa	noh-**vehn**-tah
100	cien	see-**ehn**
101	ciento uno	see-**ehn**-toh **oo**-noh
102	ciento dos	see-**ehn**-toh **dohs**
200	doscientos	dohs-see-**ehn**-tohs
500	quinientos	khee-nee-**ehn**-tohs
700	setecientos	seh-teh-see-**ehn**-tohs
900	novecientos	noh-veh-see-**ehn**-tohs
1,000	mil	meel
1,001	mil uno	meel **oo**-noh

Time

	Spanish	Pronunciation
one minute	un minuto	**oon** mee-**noo**-toh
one hour	una hora	**oo**-nah **oh**-rah
half an hour	media hora	**meh**-dee-ah **oh**-rah
half past one	la una y media	lah **oo**-nah ee **meh**-dee-ah
Monday	lunes	**loo**-nehs
Tuesday	martes	**mahr**-tehs
Wednesday	miércoles	mee-**ehr**-koh-lehs
Thursday	jueves	hoo-**weh**-vehs
Friday	viernes	vee-**ehr**-nehs
Saturday	sábado	**sah**-bah-doh
Sunday	domingo	doh-**meen**-goh